michael trading

ISBN-13: 978-1515208723

ISBN-10: 1515208729

By: Larry Jacobs

Trading futures involves significant risk of loss and is not suitable for everyone. Past performance is not necessarily indicative of future results.

TABLE OF CONTENTS

TABLE OF CONTENTS

- TABLE OF CONTENTS 2
- PUBLISHER NOTES 5
- INTRODUCTION 7
- Chapter 1- INTERVIEW WITH MICHAEL COOK 10
- Chapter 2- STRATEGY TO USE WITH NEWS ANNOUNCEMENTS .24
- Chapter 3- ECONODAY 26
- Chapter 4 - OPTIONS 28
- Chapter 5- MOVING AVERAGES 30
- Chapter 6- CYCLES 31
- Chapter 7 - SEASONALITY 32
- Chapter 8- VOLUME & VOLATILITY 35
- Chapter 9- PRICE PATTERNS 38
  - EGG OF COLUMBUS 40
  - GAPS 45

BROADENING BOTTOM FORMATION 48

BROADENING TOP FORMATION 49

RIGHT ANGLE FORMATION 50

RIGHT ANGLE DESCENDING FORMATION 51

THREE BUMP BOTTOM 52

THREE BUMP TOP 53

GAP & BOUNCE 55

DIAMOND TOPS AND BOTTOMS 56

DOUBLE BOTTOMS 57

DOUBLE TOP 58

PENNANTS 59

FLAGS 60

HEAD AND SHOULDERS BOTTOMS 61

HEAD AND SHOULDERS TOP 62

ISLAND REVERSALS 64

MEASURED OBJECTIVE DOWN 65

RECTANGLE BOTTOMS 70

RECTANGLE TOPS 71

ELLIPSE DOWNTREND 75

ASCENDING TRIANGLE 76

SYMMETRICAL TRIANGLES 78

TRIPLE TOPS 79

Chapter 10- WILLIAMS %R 82

Chapter 11- LONG WITH STOPS 84

Chapter 12- KNOW YOURSELF 86

Chapter 13 – COMMITMENT OF TRADERS REPORT 89

Chapter 14- MARKET-ANALYST 92

Chapter 15- WORLD CUP ADVISOR 93

CHAPTER 16- OTHER TRADERS WORLD BOOKS 96

CHAPTER 17 - 2015 WORLD CUP TRADING CHAMPIONSHIPS® SPONSORS: 111

ABOUT THE AUTHOR 113

DISCLAIMER 114

COPYRIGHT 117

N

PUBLISHER NOTES

Please remember that a future trading involve significant risk of loss and is not suitable for everyone, and that past performance is not necessarily indicative of future results. World Cup Championships (WCC) accounts do not necessarily represent all the trading accounts controlled by a given competitor. WCC competitors may control accounts that produce results substantially different than the results achieved in their WCC accounts. WCC entrants may trade more than one account in the competition.

For official WCC rules and information, visit
http://www.worldcupchampionships.com

Michael Cook's Convexity account in the WorldCupAdvisor.com leader-follower AutoTrade program was entered in the 2014 World Cup Championship of Futures Trading and has continued to trade after the conclusion of the competition.

Accounts trading in the WCC may be subject to commission rates different from those following the AutoTrade program. Trader's net return in the World Cup Championship is higher than the program's net return in the WCA AutoTrade program due to commission differential and the absence of subscription fees in contest calculations.

At the end of the competition through Dec. 31, 2014, the WCA AutoTrade net return was 285.4% compared to Michael's 366% return in the contest. As of May 31, 2015, the greatest cumulative percentage decline (drawdown) in month-end net equity during the life of the Convexity AutoTrade program on WorldCupAdvisor.com is -30.58% (4/30/14 to 5/31/14).

An investor must read, understand and sign a Letter of Direction for WorldCupAdvisor.com leader-follower programs before investing. This e-book contains statements of opinion.

INTRODUCTION

I want to thank you and congratulate you for downloading this book. This book contains an interview in Chapter 1 with Michael Cook, first-place finisher in the 2014 WORLD CUP Championship of Futures Trading® with a 366% net profit.

In the rest of the book I will explain to you the indicators that he said he used in the interview. You can then actually see and understand how they work. I am not going to tell you exactly how Michael Cook used the tools to make his 366% return on a $10,000 investment. That information is not public and belongs only to Michael Cook. He spent years developing his trading techniques. Here are some the indicators and methods that he said he used:

1) Moving Averages
2) Seasonality
3) Cycles
4) Seasonality
5) Price Patterns
6) William's %R
7) Long with Stops
8) Commitment of Traders Report

All of the charts in this book are produced using my favorite charting software Market-Analyst®. I have also arranged for you to get a trial so that you might have the chance to actually work with these indicators with a live charting platform; See Chapter 14 on how to access your FREE trial.

You will also be able to download the video presentation that I personally created so you can see how these indicators can be setup and followed in a step-by-step manner. You can access them here:

http://www.worldcupadvisor.com/MichaelTrading.html

After you understand how these indicators work, I would then recommend that you go to WorldCupAdvisor.com and consider following Michael Cook's trades. You can request more information here.

http://get.worldcupadvisors.com/convexity_ebook/

You will be able to automatically mirror his trades in your own brokerage account with World Cup Leader-Follower AutoTrade™ service. You will also be able to see what his trade looks like on your own charts and better understand why he made the trades. There are no long-term commitments. You can go month-by-month.

For more information about World Cup Advisor, go to Chapter 15.

Next go to Chapter 1 to read the interview with Michael Cook. As you read the interview, please remember that substantial gains cannot be made without taking substantial risk of loss. Futures trading should only be undertaken with risk capital – that is, capital you can afford to lose. Always consider whether trading is appropriate for you in light of your experience, objectives, financial resources and risk tolerance.

Chapter 1 - INTERVIEW WITH MICHAEL COOK

Michael Cook

Larry: You were the winner of the 2014 World Cup Championship of Futures Trading® with a net gain of 366%. Can you explain how you were able to do that?

Michael: Trading a competition account is very different than other forms of trading, it is far more aggressive. The World Cup has a 30+-year history and it has taken a greater-than-200% return performance in order to win most years. As it turned out, this year was both tough and unusual in that it was so close and it ended with the top three competitors gaining a greater-than-300% return. I didn't know until the day after year-end that I had in fact won it, a single trade going well or badly for any of the leaders could have changed the final results.

As for this year specifically, I have a process I use when I develop new strategies and the final stage of that testing process is to live-trade the strategy in very small size to see that the live-trade results match the real-time testing results "walking forward," just to see I haven't missed anything before I begin trading it properly. As I was completing the work on some strategies I was ready for this final live testing phase and as the results on paper had looked very promising, I decided to kill two birds with one stone and enter an account in the competition live-testing these strategies. So this year was interesting in that I had not even intended to enter and only began trading the account about April, it was almost an accidental entry.

Larry: What about indicators, do you use them?

Michael: Yes I do use indicators but I would say that traders frequently get far too hung up on them. There are two major problems that tend to occur; firstly people are looking for the Holy Grail indicator, the indicator that works in all scenarios. Of course, this is a waste of time as such an indicator does not exist. Secondly, they look for confirmation from multiple indicators. This is perfectly valid, but only if the indicators use independent variables such as time, price and volume. Using a collection of indicators such as RSI, William's %R and Stochastic will obviously confirm each other, they measure pretty much the same phenomena using the same inputs.

What I attempt to do is to take a step back and think about what I am trying to achieve. Just as an example, take Williams %R which can be quite effective in the right scenario, but the scenario is key. A high value is a good buy signal as a breakout indicator in a trending market or exactly the same value a good sell signal as a counter-trend indicator in a non-trending market. So it needs to be used in conjunction with something showing whether the market is trending or not trending.

I tend to develop my own indicators, such as starting with %R and then combining it with a volume element to indicate future trend

/ range bound activity. The last thing I would want to do is sell a high value %R reading after a series of abnormally small trading range days, such a market is obviously set up for a breakout.

In general I like very simple indicators that I can immediately look at and understand what market phenomena they are tracking or predicting. It has to make sense, not just look pretty on a few well-chosen examples.

Larry: On moving averages what setting do you use?

Michael: I use them in a couple different ways, I like some of the work of Linda Raschke, where 7 or 8 bars above a 5-period Simple Moving Average tends to indicate a continuation move of at least 4 or 5 more bars. At that point you run straight into the work of Tom DeMark who is another analyst I greatly respect, indicating a move that long, albeit measured in a slightly different way, is setting up for a reversal. No one said trading was easy!

One of the first traders I worked with back in the 1990s was very good but also a little impatient with some of the more pretentious trading theories. He would tell me to just look at the price graph and if it started at the bottom left of the screen and ended at the top right, the market was clearly in an uptrend. Moving averages are a good way for a computer to recognize that type of market. Lots of price bars above the moving average indicate the market is trending up and vice versa.

I will say I never use moving average cross overs. Testing these lasted only about an hour before I gave up.

Larry: Do you use any fundamentals?

Michael: Not a great deal. I used them more when I was trading for banks as a market maker and I found out that I did not like them, I just happen to be more technically minded. Timing trades with fundamentals is always horrendous, it is just so hard to get that timing exactly right.

The obvious key fundamental since '08 and '09 is the very low interest rate environment and liquidity conditions engineered by the central banks of various countries. That fundamental has swamped all others for the last 5 years or so and I have to think that will come to an end at some point. This does have very important implications on data selection for testing strategies if there is an expectation of a very different environment going forward.

But other than that general macro-economic awareness, I would not use fundamentals on any specific trade.

Larry: What about cycles or seasonality?

Michael: Seasonal influences I have used in the past and I am probably going to try something with them again, I think that there is some potential there, particularly with commodities. Certain types of seasonals are far stronger than others, such as those that are reflected across several expiration cycles over roughly the same period being examined. Products like grains and meats obviously do have seasonal tendencies, much more so than financials.

The question is how to deal with the results; how do you structure trades where some of the moves can be quite significant but also where the draw-downs can be aggressive in counter-seasonal years? I do have some ideas on that; seasonal may well be a part of next year's competition entry.

Cycles definitely have their place, however, I find price cycles too difficult, particularly when trying to predict highs and lows. I do believe that the markets cycle in other respects though, for example high closes in price bars tend to cycle into low closes and back again. Similarly low-range days cycle to higher range and back again, there is a natural cycle for all those things. There are exceptions but I think these are tradable phenomena.

For those scenarios, I try to develop indicators that highlight significant expansions in volatility. I believe volatility is the key variable underpinning trading success, it is more important for short term traders than direction. If the markets don't move much it is going to be hard to make money, it is that simple. Cycles in their most general form are useful.

Larry: So if something blows up one day with a lot of volatility you look at it very carefully?

Michael: Yes, certainly, any significant change in volatility presents all sorts of opportunities. I have not really been able to develop something that is effective at predicting a collapse in volatility. You can develop indicators that will indicate forthcoming higher volatility days and I have done that, but I have not yet been able to nail down something for extremely high volatility days, the explosion days such as the Flash Crash or Black Monday 1987 or similar, ahead of time.

Larry: Do you also look at volume?

Michael: Yes I do. In the futures market there are not that many independent data sources. With stocks you have many good things to use such as, market breadth & tick data, whereas in futures you have price, volume, open interest and time (i.e. cycles) and related market data such as option volatility. That is pretty much it; everything else is feeding from one of those primary sources so yes, I do try to use volume.

Volume can be quite a good indicator for coming volatility and it is independent of price. That is the key thing. Sometimes you see high volume on a high-range day and sometimes on a low-range day. Each of those is telling you something quite important.

Larry: What about price patterns?

Michael: Yes, I use those a lot. I use pattern setups with impending predicted volatility. I am much more inclined to use price patterns than indicators.

Larry: What about Elliott Wave?

Michael: No, I don't use that as intuitively it doesn't make sense to me. I would qualify that with the fact that I have not really done much work on it. It would be pointless for me to pursue it as I strongly believe you have to have conviction in anything you use, or you won't maintain trading discipline with it when the going gets tough.

I think people have problems with Elliott Wave as the eyes are adept at seeing patterns. Unfortunately they are so adept at this that they often see patterns that are not necessarily there. Think of optical illusions or the artwork of MS Escher as examples. So in a graphical way you always have to guard against your mind playing tricks on you, and Elliot Wave levels strike me as being a prime candidate for these sorts of issues.

Larry: What about Gann. Do you use it?

Michael: No and I would say for the same reasons as my response on Elliot Wave. I think Gann is another prime candidate for looking good on graphs but being very hard to justify with rigorous statistical examination. I haven't really done the work on either of these but I know I wouldn't have great faith in them and so I would have real problems maintaining trading discipline with them in tough times.

Larry: What about commitment of traders report?

Michael: Yes, I have looked at that in the past. There is some mileage there, Larry Williams is obviously the great proponent of this and he has done some very interesting work on it. I think there is something there but, similar to seasonal tendencies, the efficacy is going to be higher in the products with more cohesion between the participants in the particular market. By that I mean markets such as the softs, meats and grains. I don't think it works that well with the S&P or currencies as there is just too much going on, too much arbitrage activity and too many different types of players. I do look at it and it is on some of my screens with pure commodities, I tend to ignore it for the financials.

Larry: What commodities did you trade to win the contest?

Michael: The things I was testing were short-term options which did seem to work out well; those were predominantly in financials such as currencies. I also traded some short-term models which I had previously developed such as crude oil, soybeans and natural gas. Lastly there were a few discretionary trades in products like VIX but I tended not to do many of those.

Larry: How long do you hold a position?

Michael: I try not to day trade for two main reasons. Firstly, I am in the Australian time zone which would make day trading very difficult to execute as I go to bed as the market in Chicago opens and I wake up as the market closes. Secondly, I don't think day trading is the sweet spot for profitability.

I do have various fully automated trading systems and there are exceptions with these to the day trading rule, for example I do have a natural gas system that tends to get in early in the day and exit at the close. That is unusual for me but the results were very good so I trade it, but generally I don't day trade. The vast majority of day trades I do are when I have entered a trade but got stopped out. That is an unintentional day trade but those trades certainly happen!

I believe you need time to generate reasonable p&l and make sure you significantly exceed transaction costs. I find swing trading with duration between 2 to 5 days to be much better. With option trading I do some trades lasting two weeks or more.

Larry: How does this work with World Cup Advisor where people follow you?

Michael: I don't think the trade duration question hugely affects the work with World Cup Advisor, but working with WCA can affect trading in several other ways.

One of the things I like about WCA is that they insist that everyone is in it together, that everyone needs to get the same or better fill as the lead account whenever it trades. This means that there are some mechanical constraints such as limit orders are not allowed as those would risk split fills where some followers get the filled and others do not. I have had some difficult experiences with that over the years. So for order type, everything has to be a market or stop order. That doesn't make a significant difference to me as that is actually how I trade anyway.

World Cup accounts also slightly restrict the products that can be traded. If you are trading large numbers of contracts there are some products where it would not be practical to execute without incurring prohibitive slippage penalties. I probably would not trade lumber or orange juice outright in a World Cup account but then again, I don't trade those types of products much anyway. World Cup does have some very good execution brokers who have been very helpful to me so they also mitigate these liquidity effects as much as humanly possible.

Larry: What news or charting services do you use?

Michael: I don't use news services at all, most of the news is happening when I am asleep and I have no wish to take marginal trades as I try to react to the news.

This is also one of the advantages of having worked on institutional trading desks in that I am acutely aware of the strengths of such desks, as well as their weaknesses. The strength is the magnitude of the resources such desks have in terms of trading ability, analysts, speed of reaction and infrastructure. Their biggest weakness is that they more than likely have to trade whereas someone in my position does not. So reacting to the news would put me head-to-head with the trading desks. That is a losing proposition and a losing one by quite a margin. Eliminating emotion and "noise" as far as possible by automation and patiently and carefully choosing my entry and exit points plays to my greatest strength and their greatest weakness.

I use Econoday for keeping an eye on when significant numbers are due out. If I see a few weeks in advance that there is a central bank announcement coming and there is a decline in volatility going into that announcement that would be an interesting possible setup. Figures and speeches can obviously be a catalyst of price movement and I quite like to structure trades around those.

As for charting, I use eSignal, which is good for some things, but the system I use the most is Genesis Trade Navigator Platinum, which is also the system I use for auto trading. I end up speaking to the Genesis guys almost every week on something and their customer service is what you would like to expect from all your service providers but unfortunately you don't often get. I know that sounds a like a little sales job and I don't have any link with them, I just happen to think they are exceptionally good.

Larry: You like to make you own indicators?

Michael: Yes I do, one reason is because by the time you develop something you know it backwards and you know everything about it because you are the one that designed it. I am sure that Wells Wilder thought the same thing about RSI. I doubt he was trying to be famous and create this thing that everyone would use; my guess is his primary driver was simply to develop a useful tool.

I agree with Tom DeMark in that I don't see much point in indicators if you don't even know what it is they are measuring. Indicators are not just to draw pretty lines on screens. You need to know what they are actually going to show you, so yes I do develop my own indicators.

For example, I know that I have one indicator that is pretty similar to one Larry Williams developed. We both have exactly the same view on volatility and I think we agree on how the market behaves with regards to this factor. It took me a half a day with my programmer to come up with a good indicator for predicting volatility expansion and I know it backwards because it is mine. I think that if I put Larry's and mine on the same chart if it may well pinpoint similar days or weeks. I am not totally sure as I have never done the exercise, but that would be my guess.

Larry: When you develop your indicators do you back test them?

Michael: Yes and no. I would tend to incorporate an indicator into a strategy and that strategy would then be tested.

As I mentioned before, the problem with indicators is they only work some of the time and it is the market conditions that the indicator is being tested in that will determine its effectiveness.

For instance, we all know that at some point markets trend, generally around 25% of the time, depending on how you do your measurements. In those situations, a trend type indicator is going to work well. In the other 75% of the time, a trend indicator will perform poorly. Such an indicator is simply not going to work when the market is not trending in a given timeframe.

When you incorporate an indicator in a strategy you are trying to identify those periods when it will work. So in effect at that point you are doing a test. You are taking those lumps of data that you think it would be valid for. That would be when the strategy is taking into position.

Larry: Is there any way to know if the market is trending?

Michael: That is a very big question – show me someone who has that question completely nailed and I will show you a successful fund manager right there.

If you look at a price graph and it starts at the bottom left and it ends at the top right you're in an uptrend so don't get so busy with indicators that you miss the obvious. If I took a graph and showed it to a twelve-year-old and asked them "up or down" they would probably make a pretty good job of it.

Of course the difficultly is that the assessment is being done after the fact. So if you are in an uptrend, you know that is going to change at some point but you might as well stay with it in the meantime. I say that as someone who absolutely does not regard themselves as a trend follower, but even non trend followers need be cognizant of underlying market conditions.

Larry: What would you advise traders to do to be successful?

Michael: That's another big question. Many of the World Cup winners talk regularly amongst themselves, we all met face-to-face at various award ceremonies and I do at least a call or two a week with previous winners based in the U.S., Italy and New Zealand. A lot of things that come up in those conversations are errors to be avoided, so maybe the question is just as much what to not do in order to be successful.

Many of the things we come up with we have learned not to do but all that means is that we have progressed on to a completely different set of problems that must be tackled.

Key things are discipline and knowing yourself and knowing what you will stick to and, probably more important, what you will not. So often in trading you will find that the trade you hate the most is the one that will make you money. It has happened to me many times.

Trading has a lot of psychological challenges and it can really pull you down if you are losing money. So how do you carry on putting in the orders to make sure you do the trade when the correct set up presents itself each time, every time? You need to come up with something that works for you. Psychological challenges in trading aren't really what affect you emotionally but what affect your discipline for consistency.

I think traders, particularly new ones, tend to obsess about three things and they are right to obsess about three things; the problem is that they are the wrong three things. What I think they should concentrate on are exits, money management and psychology in ascending order of importance. What I think they actually obsess about are entries, entries and entries!

Chapter 2- STRATEGY TO USE WITH NEWS ANNOUNCEMENTS

Trading news can be very profitable if you can forecast the way prices are going to move. Price can move dramatically very quickly on the big news releases. Knowing which way prices are going to move is a very big gamble. Most traders don't trade news because it is so risky. Most traders get whipsawed when prices move down very quickly and then right back up. So whatever your position is, you get stopped out.

You need to look at the market in a different way than 95% of the traders out there do. There is always an opportunity whatever the market throws at you. You can profit from any trading scenario but trading the news is no doubt the hardest things to try to make money with if you don't understand how to make money with it. I am not going to go into how to understand the ins and outs of price movement, but I am going to give you an effective strategy for trading news.

The main problem with trading news is stops. Almost all traders enter a trade with a stop loss. After news hits, you don't know how big the move is going to be and where you should set stops at. Should you set a stop at a recent high or a recent low? You know that the price movement is going to go down and take the long stops out and go up and take those short stops out.

One strategy to us is to enter two different trades one of them long and the other one short. Don't use stop losses. When the price jumps up you can take profits on the long position and when the price goes down you can take profits on the short.

Before you take such a trade you need to be fully aware of the type of the news release. It must be an important new release. You need to learn how to use the site Econoday.com and then understand the important of each news release and how it will affect the market. The market needs to be in a very tight range before an important news event. This is also very important the stops must be in a tight range.

Option spreads can also be put together for strategies around news events without much risk. See the option Chapter 4 for the various option strategies.

You're trading needs to be based on market logic. You must have a strategy to trade every event. Always check back on historical prices and how each major news event affected the market. You need to understand what is happening on the chart and the news behind it.

The next chapter explains Econoday so you know what the news events are that are coming and what the experts are thinking before the news is released. You can also go back on previous news events and check out what happened on historical price charts.

Chapter 3- ECONODAY

It is very important to stay up to date with economic reports and news. Many plan their trading strategy around important news events. You need to know what is going to be released each day in economic news. You can access the publication at www.econoday.

If you click on the **Today US Announcements** it will tell you exactly what is going to happen each day in regards to as far as economic news. **Orange stars** will tell you if it is minor news (merit extra attention) and a **red star** tells you that it is important (a market moving indicator)

You can also click on the **consensus tabs** to learn what the consensus number is or what the experts are expecting.

See the next example of what Econoday.com site looks like.

Economic Events and Analysis

Week of June 1 - 5

US Calendar. The outlook for the Fed's first rate hike is centered on September and if expectations for Friday's employment report pan out, at a moderate 220,000 for nonfarm payroll, those expectations will remain intact. Jobs indicators going into the report, including ADP on Wednesday and jobless claims on Thursday, will further center attention on Friday. A sleeper for the week is motor vehicle sales on late Tuesday which will offer the first hard consumer data on May.

Global Calendar: The Reserve Bank of Australia, European Central Bank and the Bank of England hold monetary policy meetings this week. No policy changes are expected. However, an interest rate reduction is expected from the Reserve Bank of India. The U.S. Federal Reserve publishes its Beige Book in preparation for its FOMC meeting on June 16 and 17. The manufacturing and composite PMIs should give a good indication of how growth is faring mid-second quarter. Canada posts its April labour force survey and the U.S. reports its employment situation.

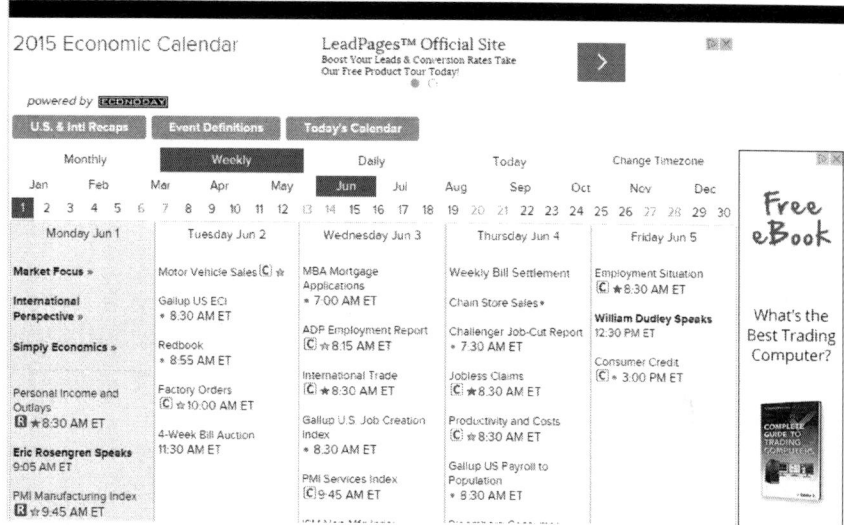

Chapter 4 - OPTIONS

Using options should be part of your strategies that you plan around every turning point in the market as well as major important reports. Options can limit your risk and maximize a return on a trade. You can learn to take advantage of options as a fantastic vehicle for trading. The following will shorten the learning curve of how options really work and limit the unlimited risk of futures contracts.

1. **Covered Call** is when you buy a futures contract and then simultaneously write a call option on the contract. You should use this strategy when you are neutral on the future's direction and want to produce additional profits through the amount of the call premium.

2. **Married Put** is when you purchase futures contracts and instantaneously purchase put options. Use this strategy when you are bullish on the futures but want to guard yourself against any short-term losses.

3. **Bull Call Spread** is when you buy call options at a strike price and then simultaneously sell calls at a higher strike price. They both have the same expiration month. You should use this strategy when you are reasonably bullish.

4. **Bear Put Spread** is where you purchase put options at a strike price and then simultaneously sells the same number of puts at then a lower strike price and both have the same expiration date.

You should use this strategy when you are bearish and expert the futures price to decline.

5. Protective Collar is when you purchase out of the money puts and then simultaneously write out of the money calls at the exact same time for the futures contract. You should use this then when you after you have had a long futures position with big gains. You can then lock in profits without selling the futures contracts.

6. Long Straddle is where you purchase both calls and options at the same strike price and expiration date. Use then when you think the futures will move a lot in one direction.

7. Long Strangle is where you purchase a call and put with the same exact maturity but with different strike prices. The put strike will be below the strike of the call. Both will be out of the money. Use this strategy when you think there will be a big movement.

8. Butterfly Spread is where you will combine a bull spread and a bear spread and use three different strikes. You purchase one call or put option at the lowest or highest strike price and then sell two calls or put options at a higher or lower strike price, then one last call or put option at a higher or lower strike price.

9. Iron Condor is where you hold a long and short position in two strangle strategies. This is a complex strategy.

10. Iron Butterfly is where you combine a long or short straddle with the simultaneous purchase or sale of a strangle.

Chapter 5 - Moving Averages

You can use moving averages as a trigger to enter the market. Use a combination of a 7-day moving average and a 5-day moving average. When the price closes about the 5 and the 7-day moving averages you can go long. When prices close under the 5-day and 7-day moving average you can sell short. But only do this when the swing chart has broken a previous high and sell short only after the swing chart has broken a previously low. See the following chart.

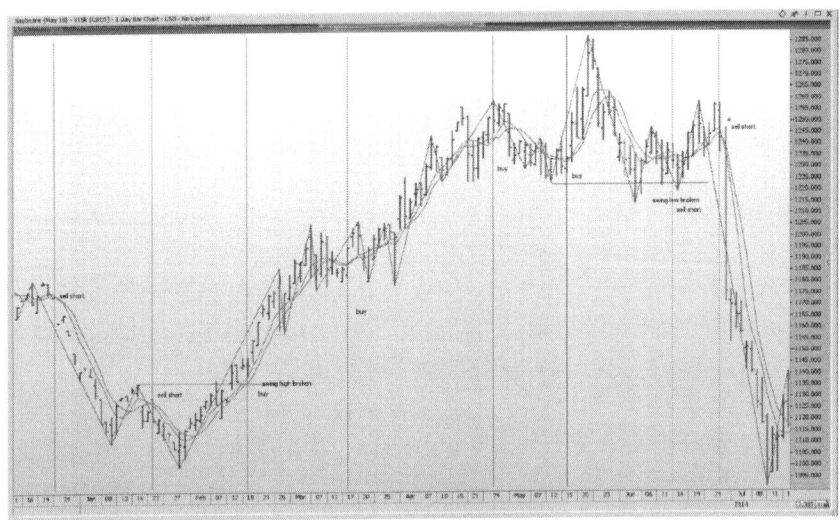

Chapter 6- CYCLES

The market does move in cycles. Sometimes it is hard to calculate them. One way is to look for a low range of sideway prices in a rectangle. When the price breakout of this range you can go with them. You can use the swing chart to find these low range rectangles. Then you can calculate a cycle of vertical lines and plot that on the chart. In the following chart I calculated the cycle to be around 66 trading days. The prices then will break out of the rectangles and go into the next cycle turn. You can use the 5 and 7-day moving averages to trigger the trades out of the rectangles. Always go in the direction of the swing lines.

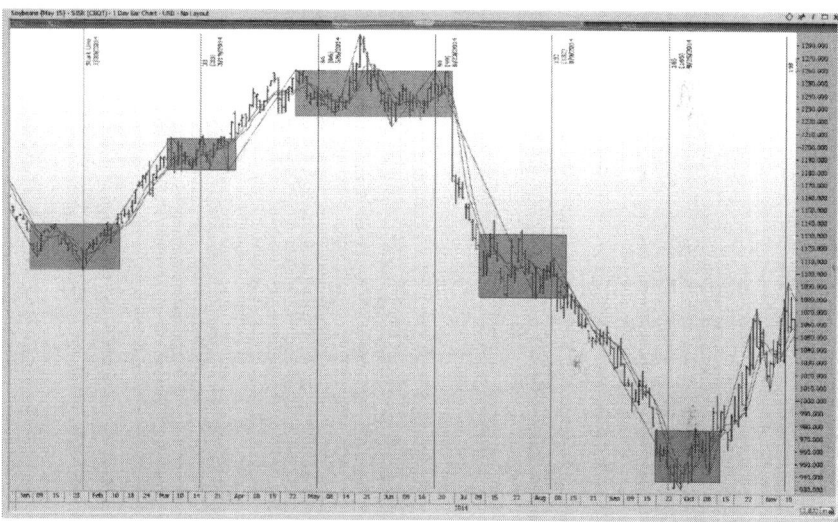

Chapter 7 - SEASONALITY

Seasonality is the study of average price movements during turning points in the span of a year.

This study essentially originated in agricultural commodity markets. The amount of grain that arrives at harvest time ordinarily drives prices down. Then the product is consumed throughout the rest of the year with increased demand prices typically rise.

This chapter will discuss the ideas behind this study of seasonality and the tool to monitor seasonal patterns.

Cycle analysis has always been a part of technical analysis and seasonality has been a part of it particularly in regard to commodities and the grain market. Supply and demand occurs with imbalances that happen during a year. The harvest pressure of grain coming to market normally drives grain prices down. It is very easy to see how seasonal influences play a major influence in prices especially in grains.

Markets are a discounting type of a mechanism and for that reason it will anticipate the seasonal changes in both supply and demand. That means that tops and bottoms in the market may occur earlier and may jump ahead of the harvest time.

Seasonal timing is not fixed and will not occur the same time each year. There are other factors such as global trade, distribution and supply and demand that also affect prices. For example, the crop production of South America and consumption worldwide can change a normal seasonality tendency.

Soybean prices usually present us with typical price cycles. The Seasonal tops do tend to occur around February, March and April and lows occur July, August and September. The beginning of the drop starts in June as you can see in the following monthly seasonality chart. In this book all charts are made with the software Market-Analyst which I feel does analysis of the markets better than most any other software.

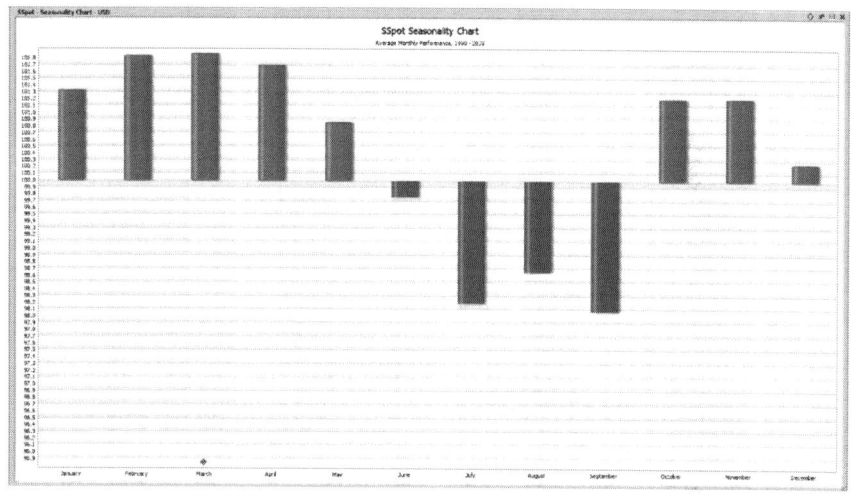

In this next chart see a daily seasonality chart. You will notice that there is a tendency of the market to turn down late June. Notice June 28th is the seasonal beginning of weakness. This weakness was foretold many months ahead of the actual fact.

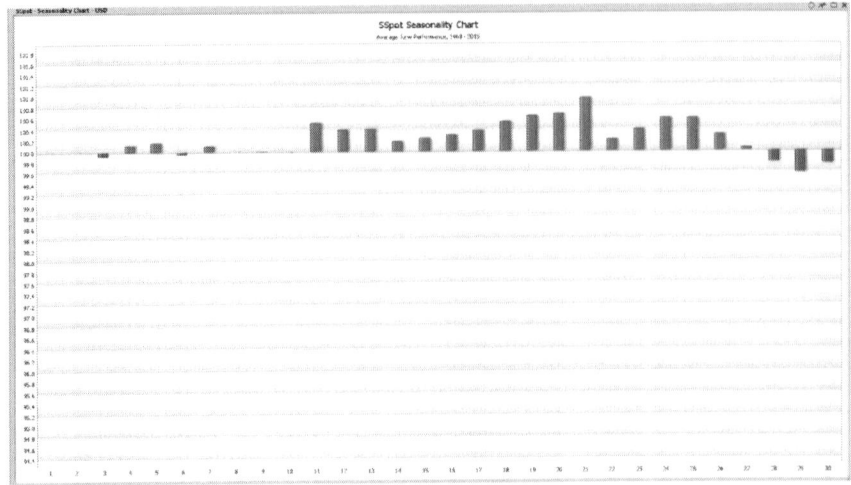

Notice on the actual price chart where the peak of the soybean's price was June 28th. This was the predicted top on the daily seasonality chart. The market turned down after that point and there was a severe drop in prices.

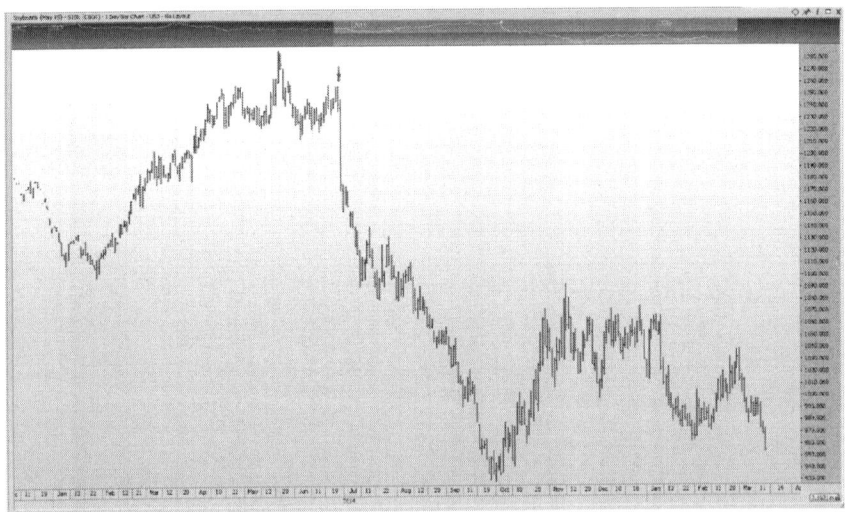

Chapter 8- VOLUME & VOLATILITY

Volume is very important as it shows the interest in a futures contract. Current volume in a futures contract relative to the prior volume does show if the interest is higher or lower than it was previously. High volume is suitable for active traders and low volume generates a lack of interest and traders should stay out of these markets.

There are three ways to use volume with price analysis.

1) Confirm trends

2) Spot price reversals

3) Confirm breakouts

Confirming Trends

Volume provides information about price. If volume increases slowly as price declines the rising volume confirms the downtrend. See chart below.

If volume increase as prices increases in an uptrend the trend is bullish.

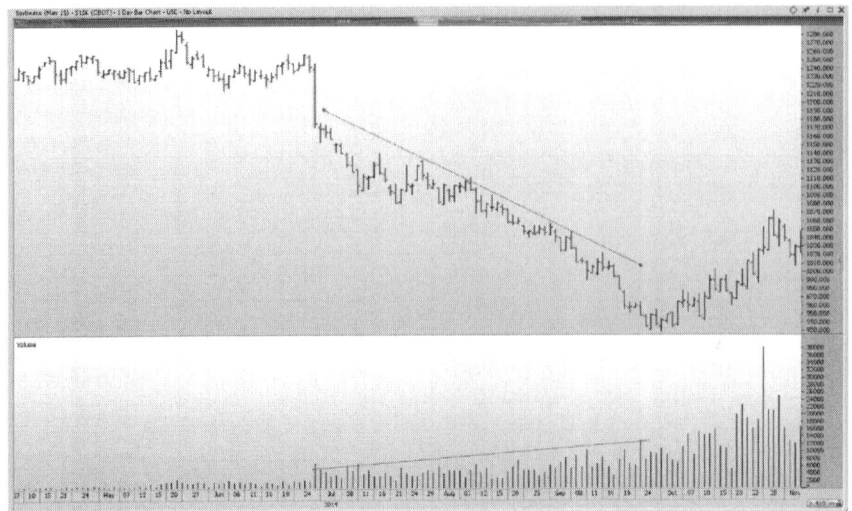

Price Reversals

When the volume spikes way above the standard volume it may indicate that the buyers or sellers are exhausted. Many times this will occur with a key reversal in the market. That is where the price goes up and then back down and closed under yesterday's high price.

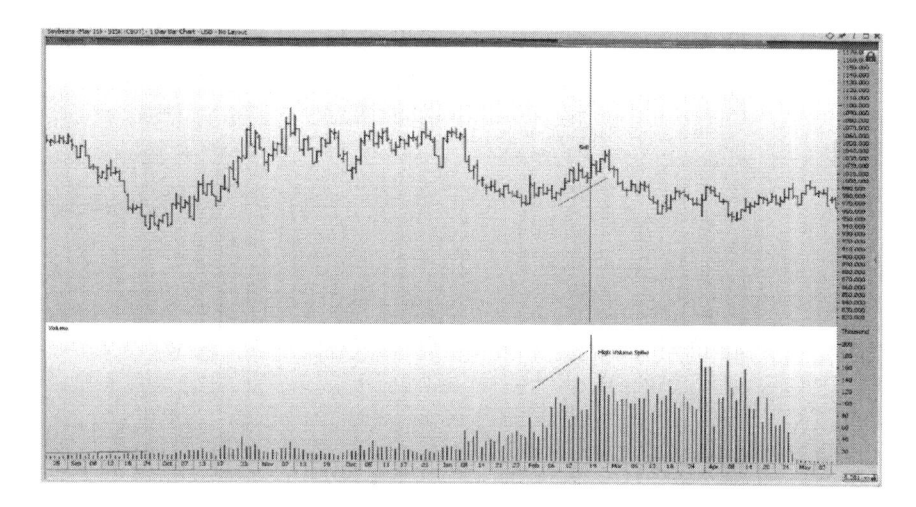

Price Breakouts

When there is major support and resistance volume can confirm a breakout. If the price has struggled in a sideways trend and has struggled to get above or below support and resistance volume can help to confirm the breakout. See the following chart.

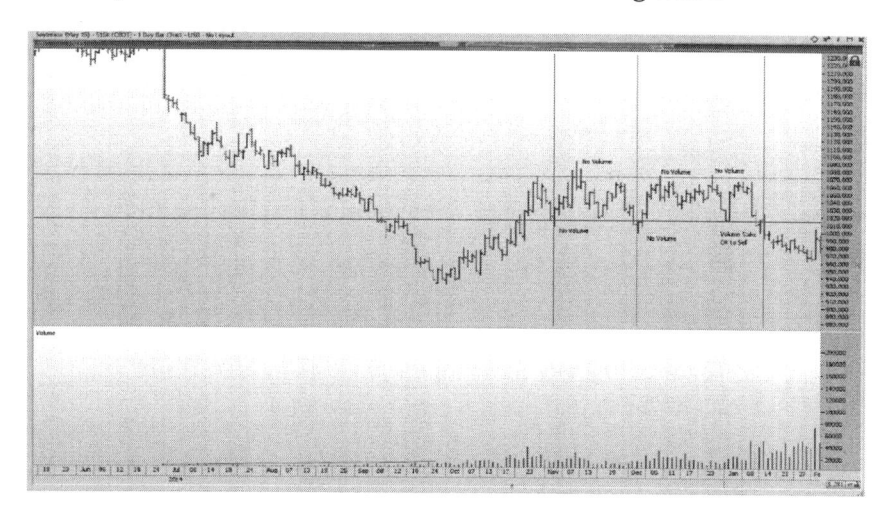

Chapter 9- PRICE PATTERNS

Day after day we visualize pictures and objects in our mind. We draw on these objects from everyday images, which we see and are absorbed in our mind and applied to our everyday activities. Instinctively we ascertain these images in our mind so that we might draw conclusions as to what they make up and how they can be used in our interaction with our daily activities.

Depending on our individual ability and wholehearted observation we can move forward to a higher level of the science of visualizing images from recurring study of them. Some people might call this practical experience. This practical experience must be combined with thought to elevate the student to a higher and keener level of expertise of recognizing objects. The more experience a person has in recognizing objects and analyzing them, the more he is apt to be successful in this endeavor.

It's almost impossible to visualize a car traveling on the highway upside down. Your past experience of seeing or driving a car has convinced you that it is impossible for a car to travel upside down, except for the possible exception of it being turned over in a moving accident.

Similar comparisons can be made is visualizing other objects and there movements. Your past experience causes your mind to restrain your ability to mentally picture hypothetical images.

In this book the reader will be taught to recognize images of patterns and ellipses and how they can be used to detect changes of trends. It is extremely important that the reader allows his mind to fully develop in this area. This can only be done with extensive study and visualizing these patterns and ellipses on a continuing basis. Repetition is the name of the game. The more you do it, the better you will get at it.

The trader must pay attention to the market. He must know when to buy and sell by watching the market's stop and go signals. Psychology plays an important part in the profits and loses of a trader. If a trader buys a security when the market is in a downtrend and experiences a loss, he must learn from it and not do the same mistake again. The pattern he visualized was incorrect and he must analyze what went wrong and not do it again. Some traders are stubborn and feel the market cheated them and they'll get their money back next time using the same signal and doubling up. The trader did not watch the stop light. The same patterns occur over and over again. The trader will only begin to be successful when he starts to pay attention and remembers the patterns whatever they may be.

EGG OF COLUMBUS

George Bayer was a famous market trader, course and newsletter writer in the 1940's. He felt it was his job was to teach those interested in how to trade the markets with strange, innate but accurate cycles. He felt that writers such as Swedenborg who had written 20,000 pages and Athenaeus who had written some 3000 pages had just scratched the surface of cycle study. He wanted to condense the study of cycles down to just a very few pages but make every page count and mean a lot. He wrote several courses and a series of newsletters.

He also felt that the people living ages ago were much smarter and wiser than anyone living in his time. He felt that he got his wisdom from studying them. He said that he didn't owe his generation a nickel's worth of thanks. He even said the current generation held him back; having to wade through all their works until his hard thinking put him on the right tract.

He felt that the forecast of what is to come, for example, in wheat or corn next year was preset and continuing. To be successful all one had to do was to try to locate the cycle and ride with it. He felt this was extremely difficult to do for the average person. He felt that each living creature on earth has its own cycle it was living in. This cycle may or may not be harmonious with the cycles of other living things. He felt that if someone's own cycle was disharmonious with stocks or commodities that person will never want to trade in them. Others whose cycles are harmonious with stocks will trade them and win.

He felt that traders get vaccinated with false opinions as to what moves the markets. This comes from newspapers, books written on the subject of market analysis and today even television. Look at CNBC. It clearly and constantly bombards the public with its opinions and the opinions of its guests. The ideas and opinions of these people are imbedded into the minds of the public and it's almost impossible to get these ideas out of their minds. The public thinks they know what affects the market. For example frost in Iowa or rain in Kansas moves wheat up and down.

In his course the Egg of Columbus, George Bayer brings up the study of Athenaeus and his study of cycles. There is a natural law which says: you'll get what is coming to you and you never will get that which is not meant for you and therefore you should be able to see quickly how marvelous nature shows itself in all things. He felt that it must be very clear that there is an interweaving of cycles. The secrets contained in Athenaeus could be written with one word or one title: Dinner Table.

He said that what can be understood from the knowledge of cycles is that the cycles of markets, of business, the life of a human being, bank accounts, trading accounts, wheat, cotton, and every commodity consists of a series of cycles, long and short, which form one whole. Links form a chain. He called these cycles serpents. The formation of these serpents is represented in things which we eat and in the rotation how we eat the various foods. He said you would not start with the roast when eating a seven-course dinner, but you begin with the Hors d'Oeuvre or Antipasto, that is with radishes, green onions, pickles, salami, anchovies, and caviar. He felt that the Dinner Table was not his ideas, but what the Ancients had known thoroughly. He felt that knowing the theory of the Dinner Table we had to know something about eating and the series in which the dishes of food were served at dinner. There is a definite sequence of how dinner should be served.

Here is the sequence of how food should be served at dinner:

1) Begin with the Hors d'Oeuvre and a cocktail
2) Next follows the soup
3) After the soup comes the fish
4) Small round boiled potatoes are served with the fish.
5) White wine is served with the fish.
6) When the fish has been eaten, we start with the roast
7) With the roast goes red wine.
8) After the roast comes the sweet stuff
9) With it should be served Champagne
10) Then we get cheese and crackers
11) Lastly we get almonds and nuts with which goes a little brandy.

He felt that not only do we have to know about how we eat dinner but also we must know about how the dinner must be disposed of.

Another important point about cycles that George Bayer brought out is that there is an interweaving of cycles. Fixed stars form distinct pictures of animals in the evening sky. These animals are running around the globe in millions. They eventually die. Don't forget that these animals perpetuate themselves throughout time. A new baby animal is born and then a parent dies later. In other words, a new cycle starts before the old one ends. Please remember this important point.

Thus what Mr. Bayer discovered is that all the markets represent full a man who lives, eats and disposes of waste matter. He felt this was an extremely important secret that he rediscovered. Mr. Bayer felt that the sooner you work your mind in to understanding such a menu and go over the various dishes and their sequence the better you will understand the cycles of the markets. The market lives on food, not food as such but pictures of food arranged in the form of a top-notch meal, which includes wine and champagne.

Therefore Mr. Bayer said that if you take any bar chart all you do is look for the Hors d' Oeuvre, then for the soup, afterwards for the fish and its fins, then for the roasted bird with its neck sticking out and even its beak from which it spits out a nut or an almond, then you have gone through the complete bull phase. You know the bull phase is over because he has to get rid of that what he has eaten and begins first to p—and then to s—and he repeats that several times, in fact he does this so often until the tongue hands out of his mouth, because he is so hungry that he must eat at once. The handing out of the tongue is the surest sign that he is cleaned from what he had eaten and you will never forget the picture of a tongue if you see one.

The size of any move depends upon the size of the tongue that sticks out. In the tongue is contained the Hors d'Oeuvre.

The following illustration is a drawing of exactly how Mr. Bayer thought a dinner course should look.

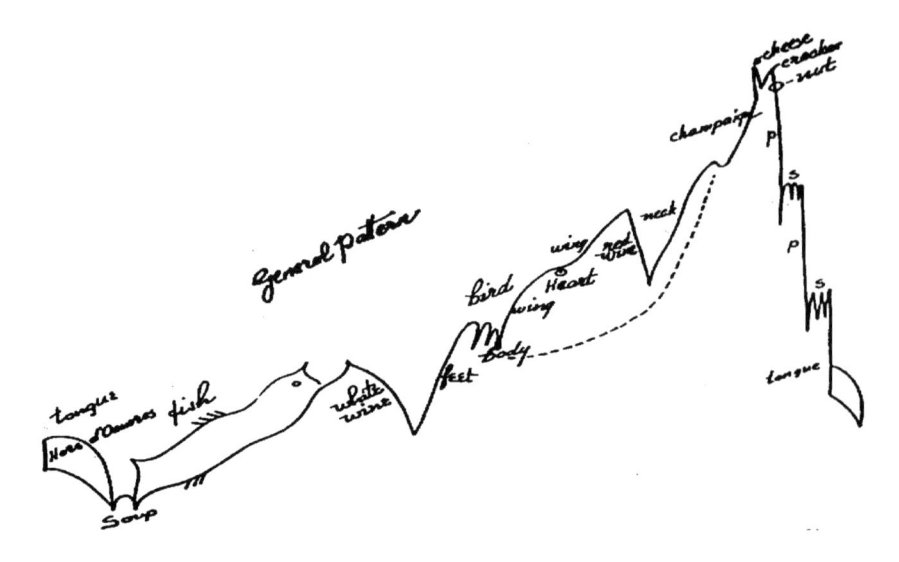

The following chart is an example of the Egg of Columbus using a daily chart of Light Sweet Crude.

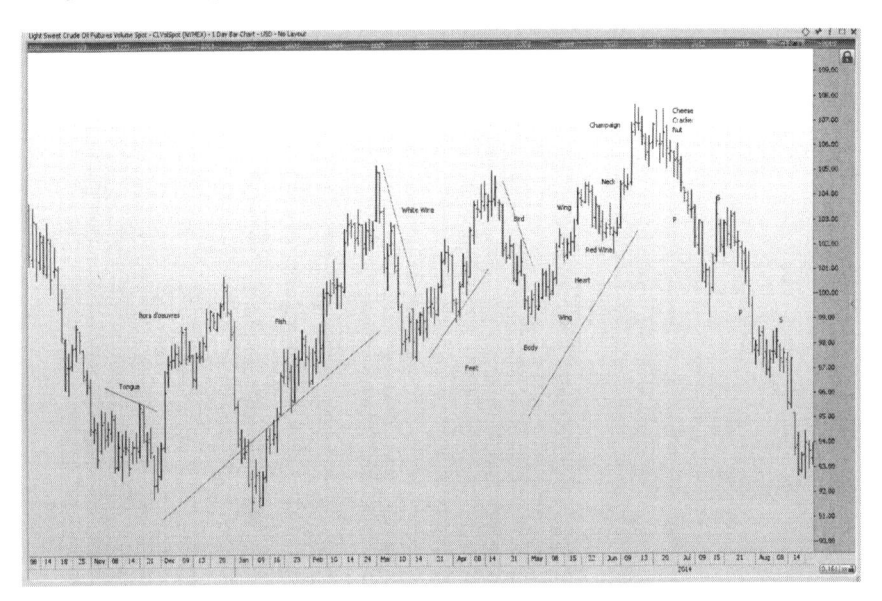

GAPS

A gap is an open space on your charts between one trading day and another. Gaps usually are something that is nothing to think about. In fact most gaps are usually closed within 1 to 3 days. Some gaps are closed several days or weeks later. Some traders use them as objectives. An open gap is many times a target for a potential move.

Breakaway Gap - When a gap occurs with velocity, it is something to watch. It's called a breakaway gap. In most cases it is the beginning of an accelerated move. The top or the bottom then must be considered as in place. The move does not start from that top or bottom but from the gap. The move starts from the bottom of the gap in a downtrend and the top of a gap in an uptrend. The move will last one of these numbers.

Midpoint Gap - The other types of gaps are the midpoint gap and the exhaustion gap. The midpoint gap occurs after a move has started. In the middle of the move it makes an open gap. From that point you can measure in the middle of the gap and project a measured move. In the following chart you see an example of a midpoint gap, which projected to an exact top.

Exhaustion Gap - Later on you also see an exhaustion gap that terminated the move of the stock.

46

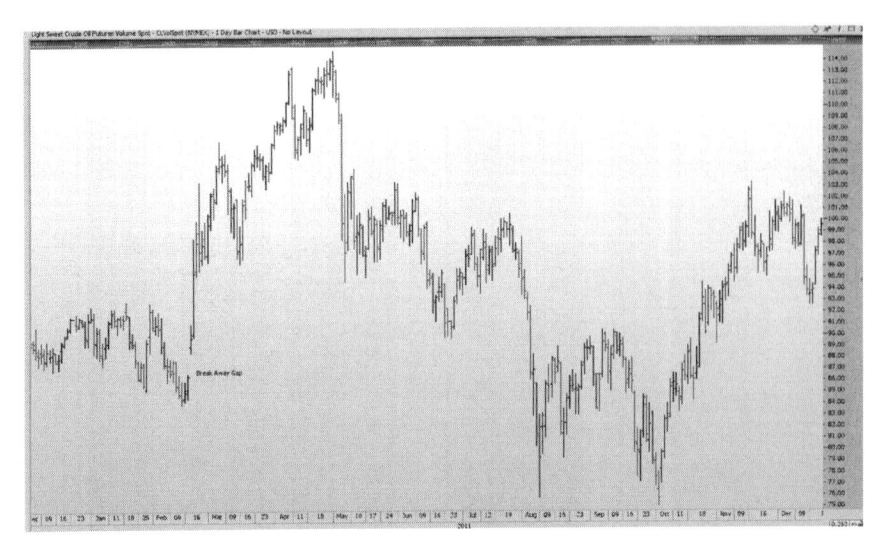

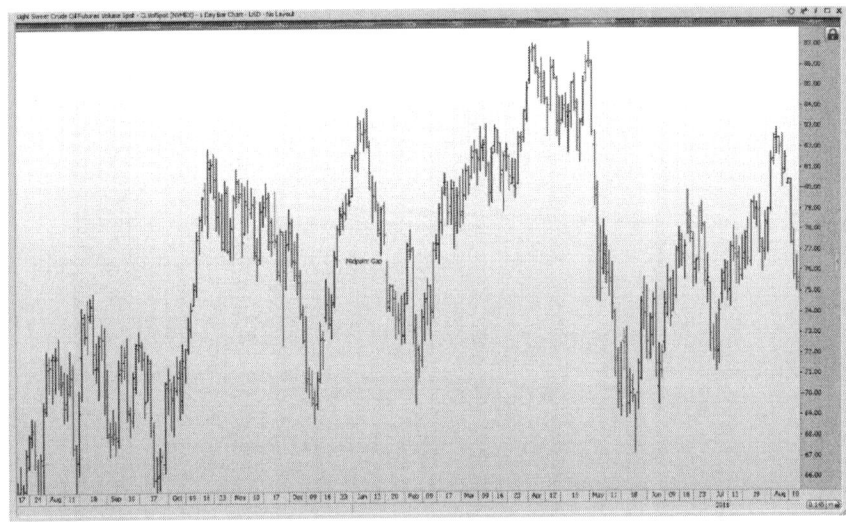

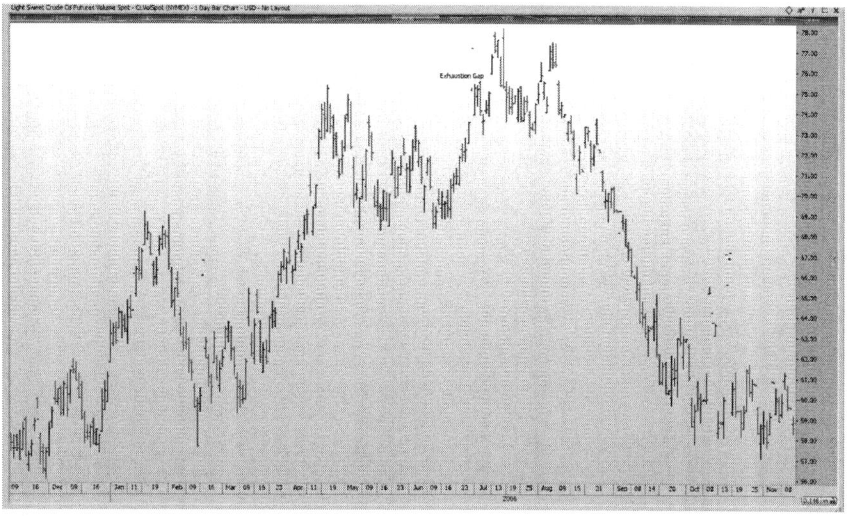
Light Sweet Crude Oil Futures Volume Spot - CL.VolSpot (NYMEX) - 1 Day Bar Chart - USD - No Layout
Exhaustion Gap

BROADENING BOTTOM FORMATION

In this formation price comes down into an expanding triangle bottom. The formation makes at least 2 higher highs and two lower lows. It must make at least four touches of the triangle. If you recognize the formation early then buy the low at point 5. Put your stop right under the low you bought at. Sell at the top of the triangle at the end of the ellipse or wait for the breakout and sell that the top of the breakout ellipse.

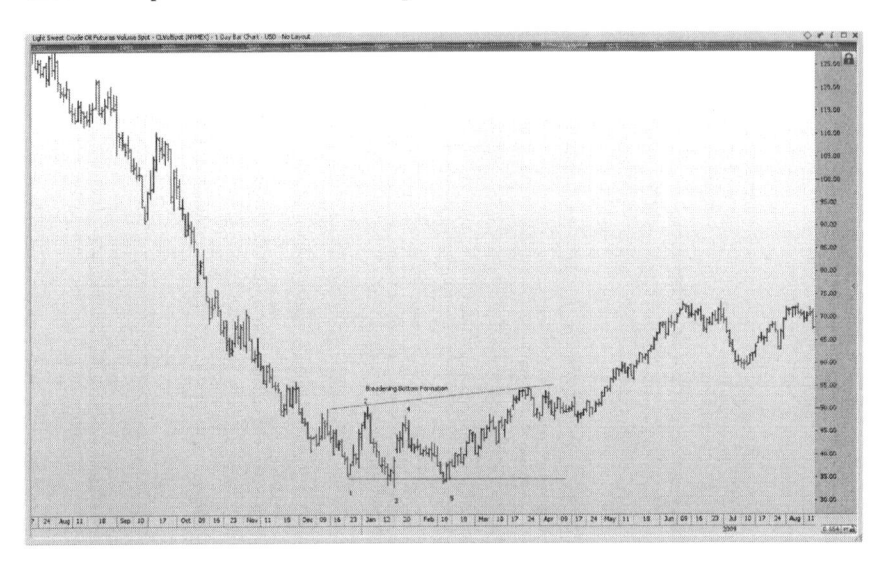

BROADENING TOP FORMATION

This type of formation is identical to the broadening bottom formation. It needs at least 4 touches of the triangle. The price should eventually breakdown out of the formation and decline. The strategy is to short at point 5 with a close stop, take profits at the bottom of the triangle or wait for the downside breakout and take profits at the bottom of the ellipse. The second strategy would be to wait for the breakout on the downside. You should then short immediately with a stop inside of the triangle. Then take profits at the bottom of the triangle.

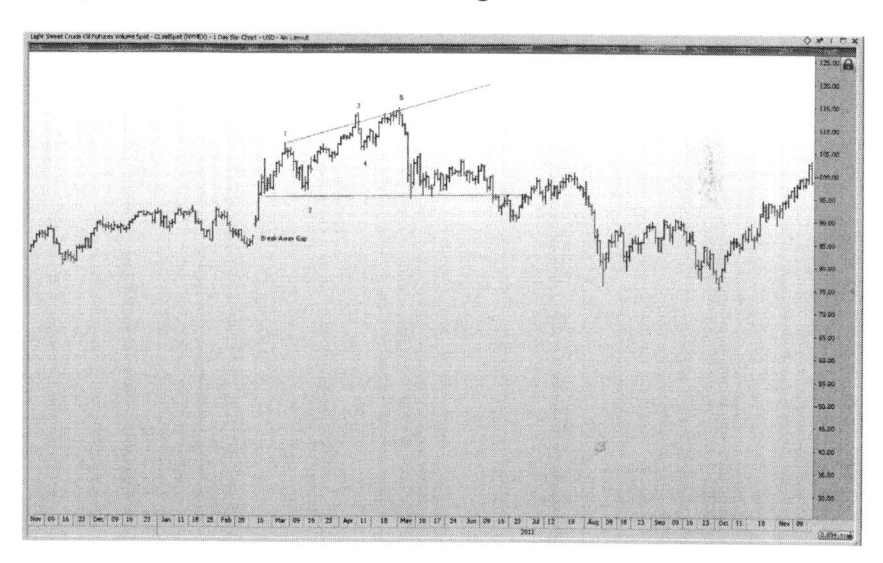

RIGHT ANGLE FORMATION

The right angle formation has a flat bottom and a rising angle top. There needs to be at least four touches on the triangle. You can buy at point 5 with a close stop. Take profits at the top of the triangle or wait for it to breakout and take profits at the end of the next ellipse. A second strategy would be to wait for the breakout and then take profits at the end of the next ellipse.

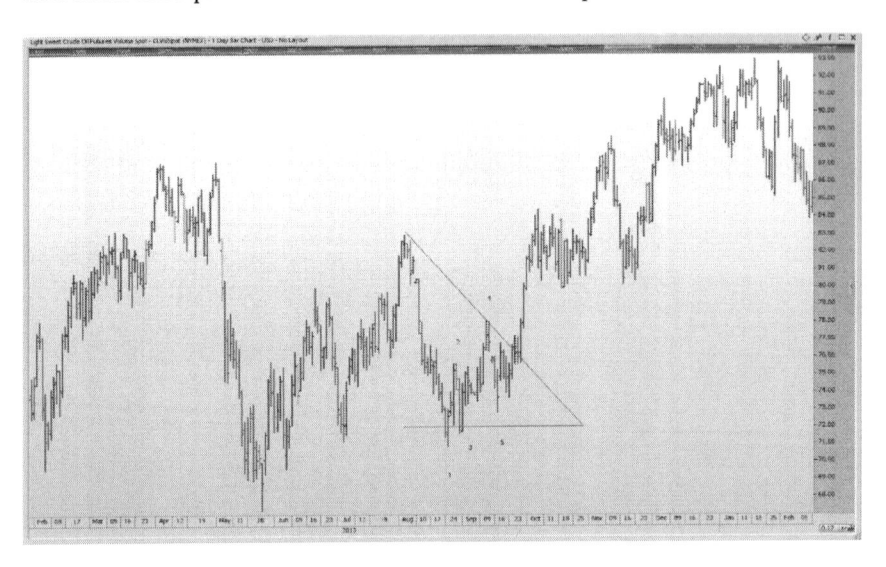

RIGHT ANGLE DESCENDING FORMATION

This formation has a flat top and a descending lower angle bottom. Again this triangle must have at least four touch points. Strategy is to buy at point 5 with a close stop. Sell at the top of the move.

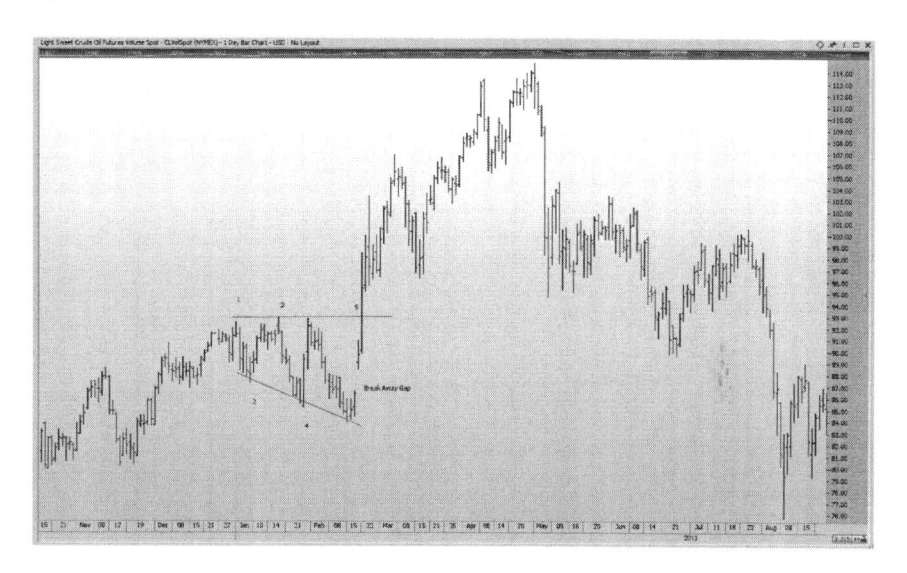

THREE BUMP BOTTOM

One of the most reliable signals is a three-bump bottom. If you see the next chart the formation always starts with two thrusts down and finally one last thrust with more power. After you have that sequence of thrusts, the market turns back to the upside again.

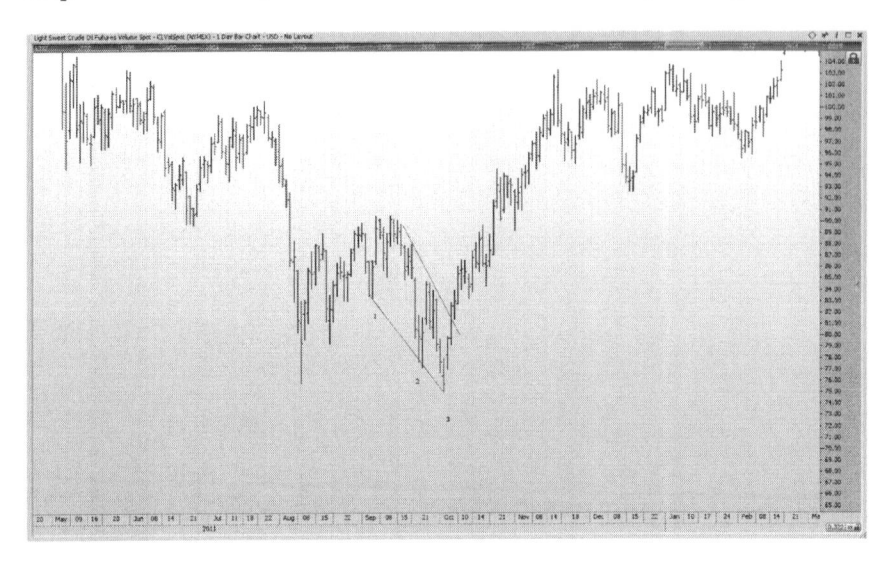

THREE BUMP TOP

Just like we had a three-bump bottom, we can also have a three-bump top. The best strategy is to try to sell the 3rd top.

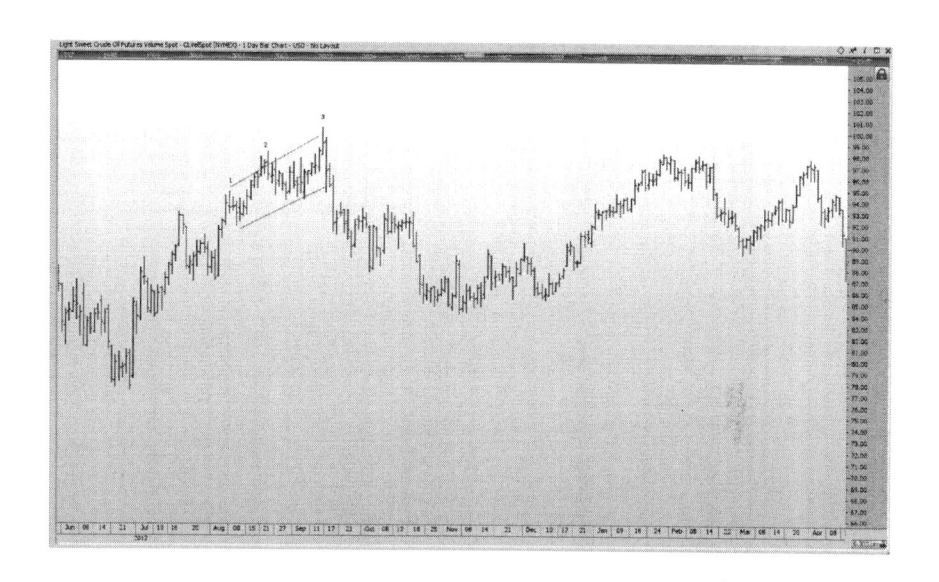

CUP AND HANDLE

The cup with handle is a formation where you have a big rounded bottom and it starts to rise then prices break out and fall back to the cup lip. The best strategy to use is to buy when prices come back to the cup lip. Follow the prices with moving stops from there on.

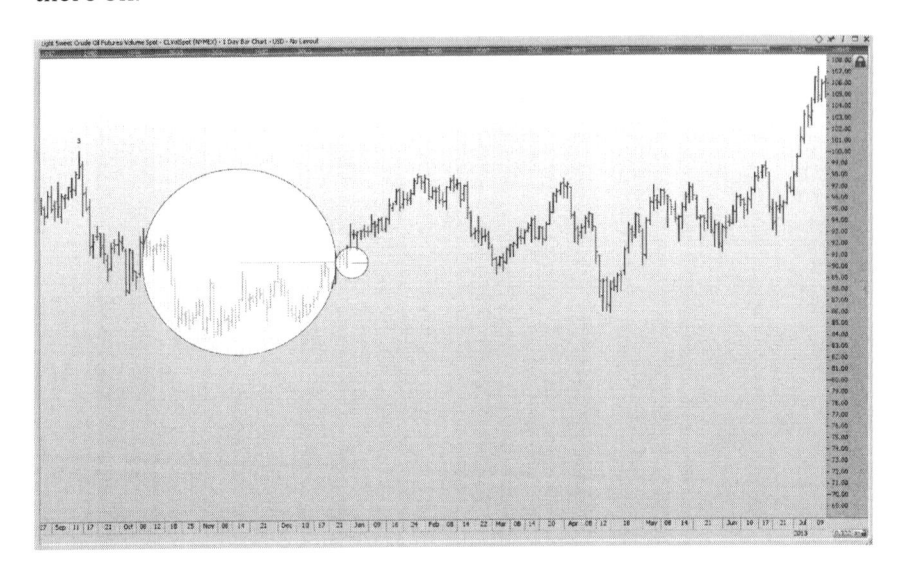

GAP & BOUNCE

One thing to look for in volatile markets is the gap and bounce. It usually occurs because of a news event. The market will gap down or up with a large space between previous day's prices. It will continue to move and have a slight reaction or recovery high in the case of a downtrend. This is where to take a position in the direction of the big gap.

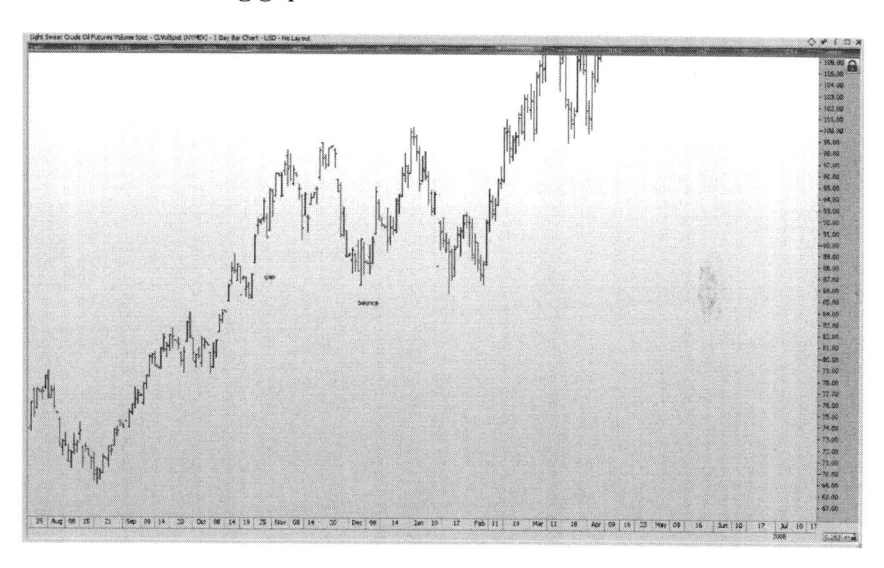

DIAMOND TOPS AND BOTTOMS

The diamond tops and bottoms occur when almost a small head and shoulders formation appears and forms inside a diamond outline. In some cases sides 1, 2, 3 and 4 are equal, but not necessary. In the case below when prices break out to the downside its objective is determined from the distance from the head to the bottom measured from the right apex. In many cases it has an expected bottom from a near term previous bottom. Strategy would be to short it when it breaks out of the diamond and take profits at its objective, the previous expected bottom line or the bottom of the ellipse.

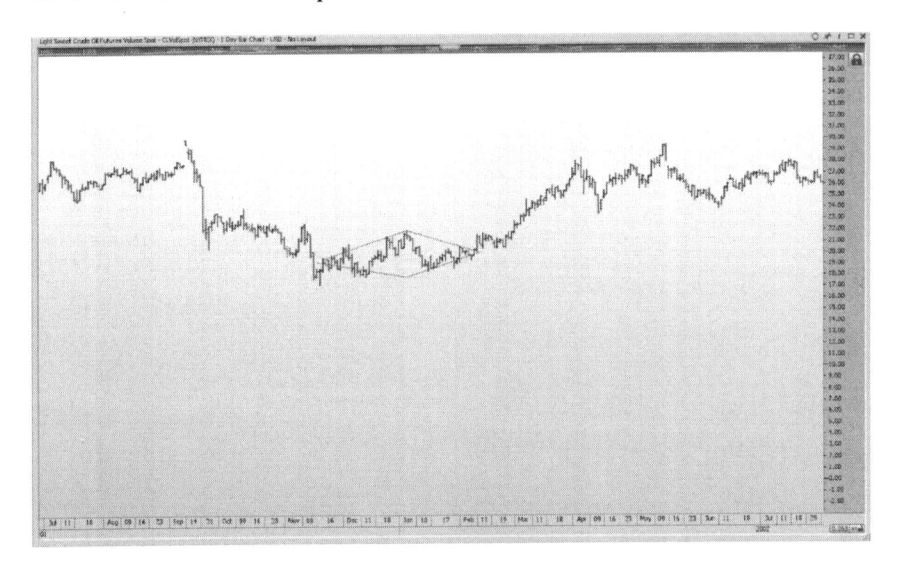

DOUBLE BOTTOMS

Double bottom occur at nearly the same level. The middle of the formation has a high and this is the confirmation line for a potential breakout. When a breakout occurs you can buy the first pull back to the breakout line. Use close stops for your protection. Your objective measurement is taken from the first bottom or second bottom to the confirmation line. Measure up again from the confirmation line the same distance.

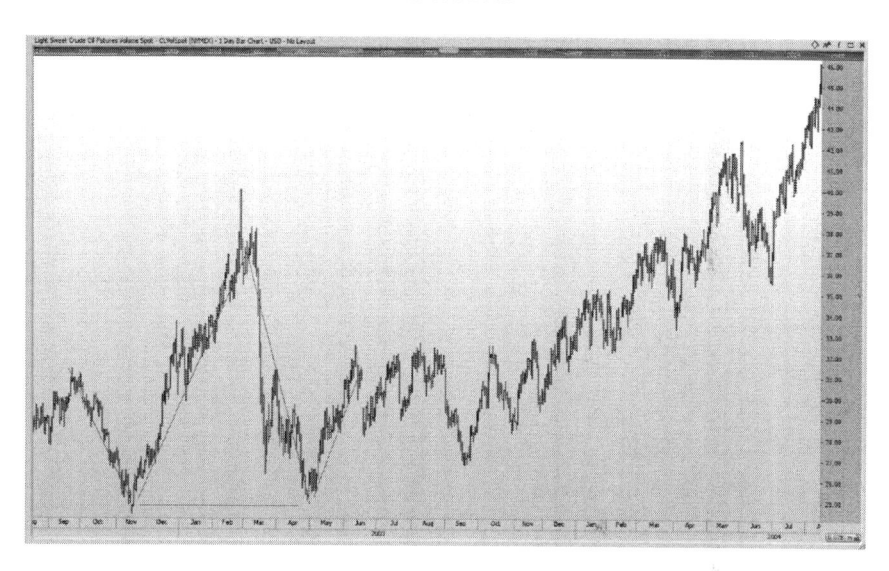

DOUBLE TOP

In this example of a double top it was very clear when it broke its confirmation line. It had an excellent pull back to short on. There was no gap, so the ellipse indicated its objective down to the previous projected low. Prices dropped rapidly down to the ellipse's objective and ended right after the exhaustion gap occurred near the bottom.

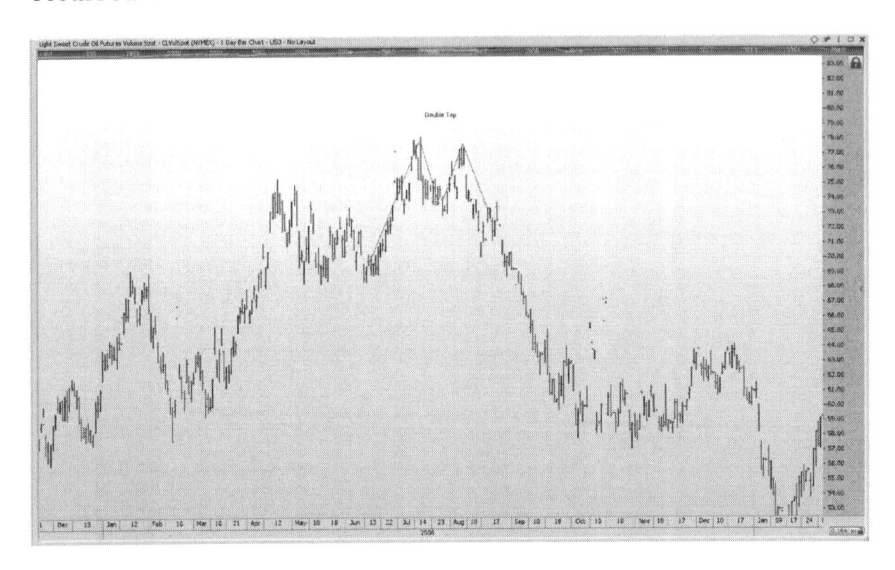

PENNANTS

These types of formations are short in duration and go the direction of the main trend. They are usually a pause in the direction. You can usually buy the breakout of the formation and sellout at the objective. The objective is measured from the start of the trend to the middle of the pennant formation. The same distance is then measured up from the same point.

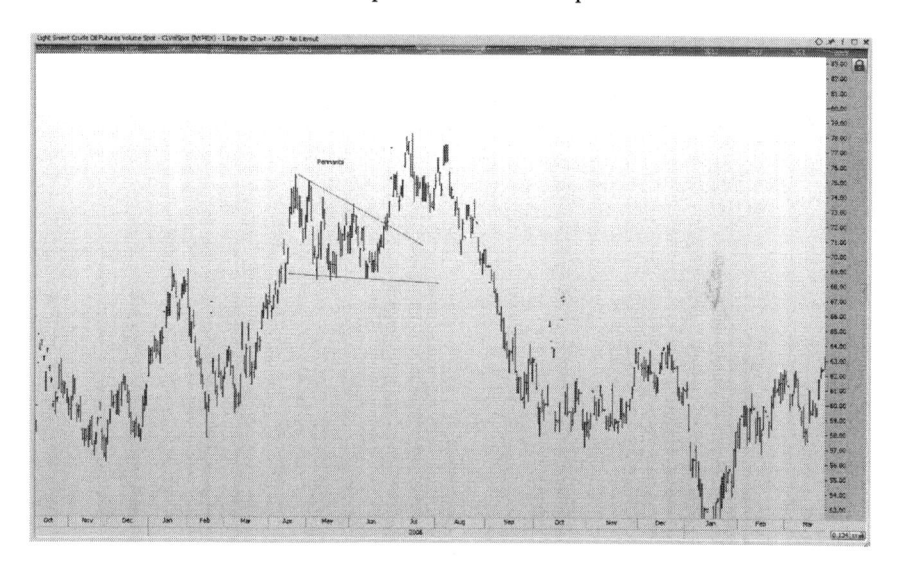

FLAGS

Flags are about the same thing as pennants. The formation comes to a point instead of being open. The measurement technique is the same. The measurement from start to the middle of the flat is taken. Then project this up the same amount to give you your objective.

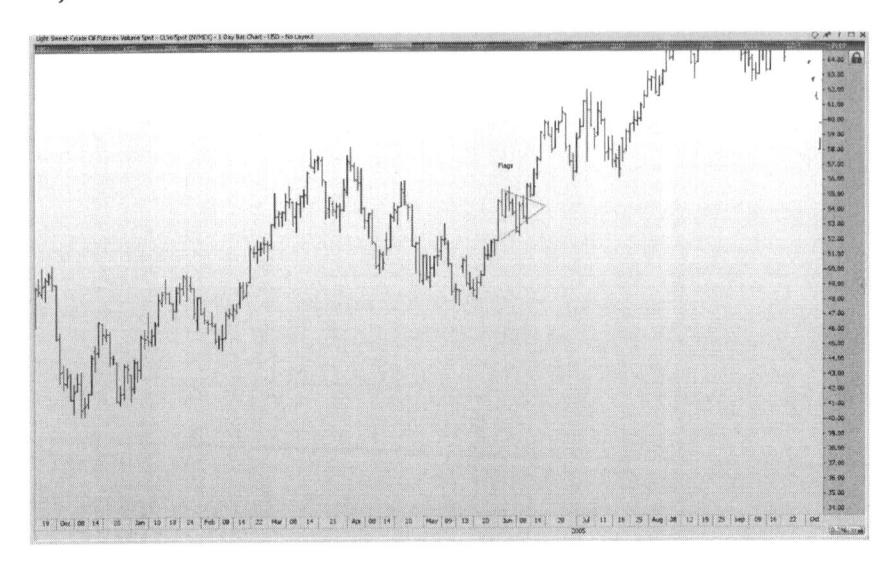

HEAD AND SHOULDERS BOTTOMS

The head and shoulders bottom is formed by three thrusts to the downside. The left shoulder and right shoulder are usually higher than the head. The neckline comes off the left shoulder high and hits the right shoulder high. When a breakout occurs it usually falls back to the neckline or even below it sometime. The stop should be placed under the support of the bottom right shoulder. The objective after the breakout is the distance of the head from the neckline forecasted up the same amount. The previous high is also an objective as is the objective of the ellipse formed after the gap occurred from the buying pullback.

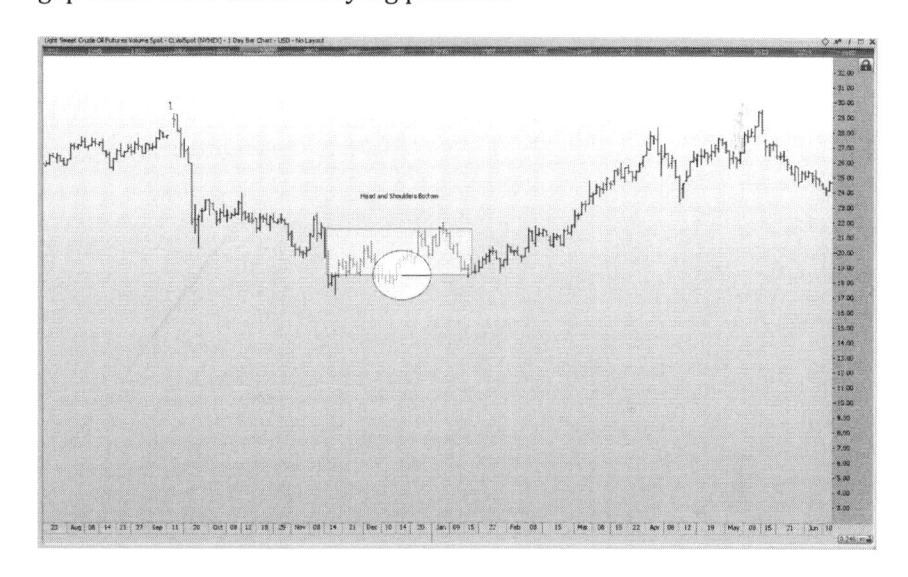

HEAD AND SHOULDERS TOP

In this case a head and shoulders top formed with three failing thrusts up. The head was higher than the left or right shoulder. The price fell back to the neckline several times. Strategy would be too short after the break under the neckline. Keep stop close. Objective would be the head and shoulders objective, the previous near term low objective.

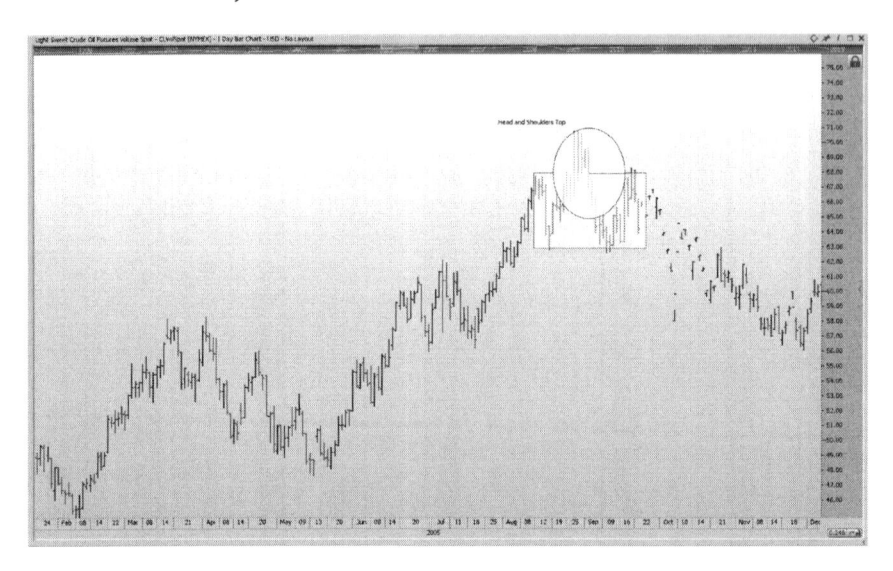

INSIDE BAR

The inside bar is a bar with a price range narrower than the day before. You must wait for the direction of the breakout and go with it. It usually produces a small move.

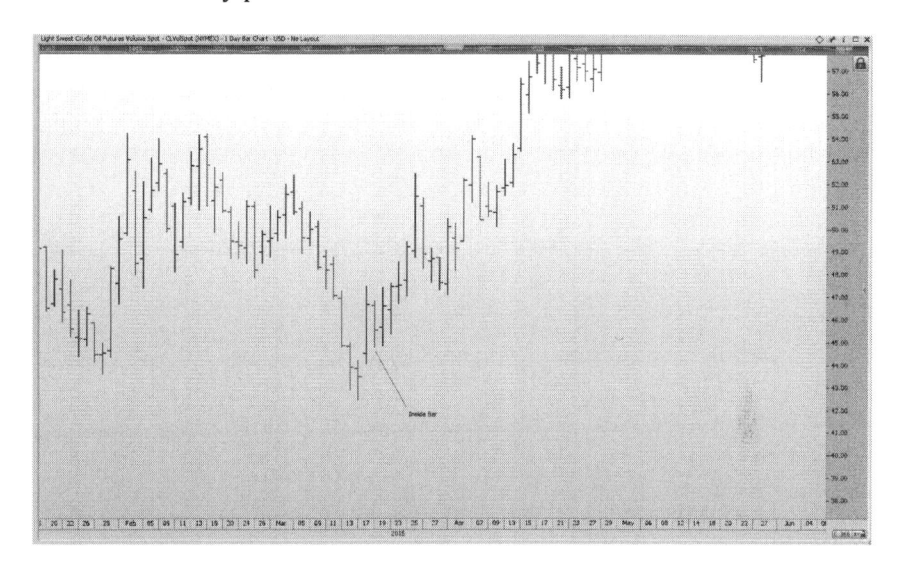

ISLAND REVERSALS

This is a formation where prices gap up into and then gap down out of. The formation is rather rare. When you do find one it is usually news driven. You should watch carefully for gaps to use ellipses on to measure objectives from.

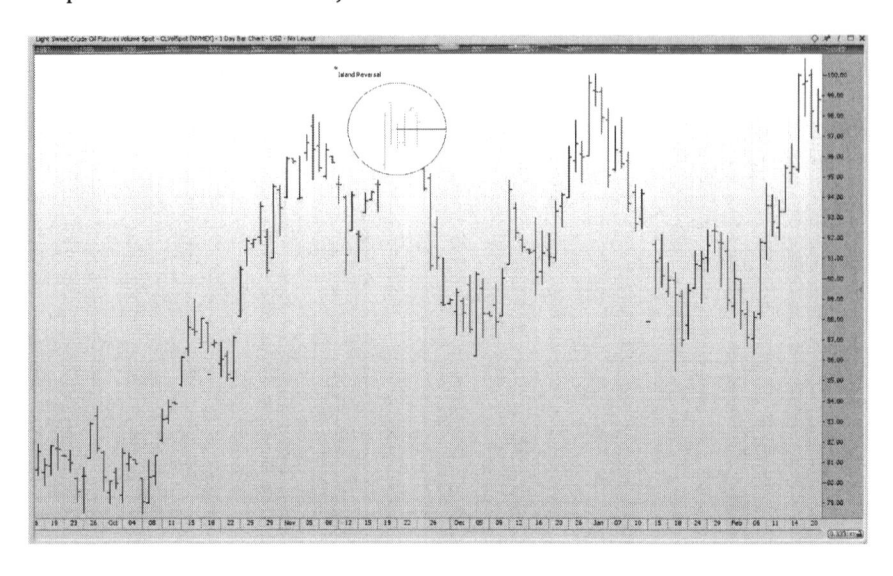

MEASURED OBJECTIVE DOWN

Using measured objectives if fairly reliable. You merely take the first move down A to B and wait for the reaction to C. You then add the same distance A to B on to C on the downside. You also tie into the projection of the previous low, which is near the same measured move.

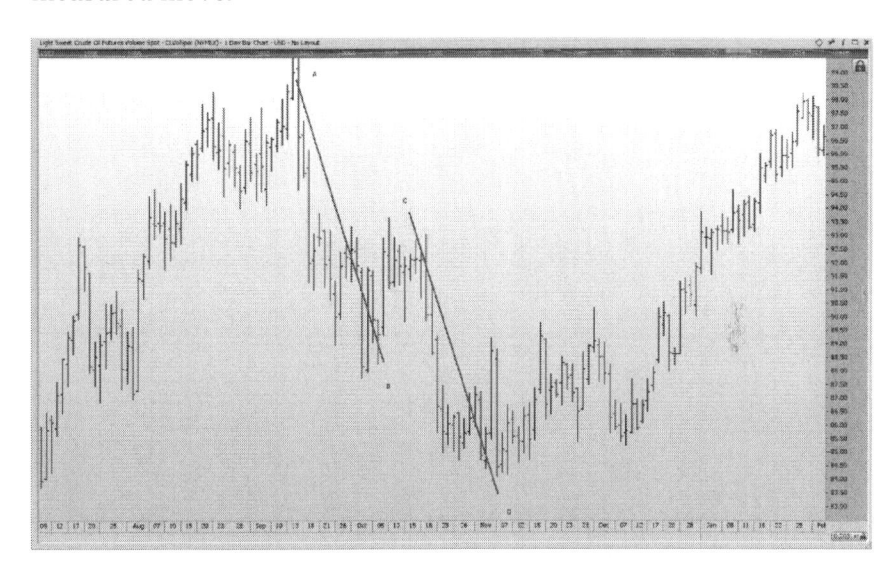

MEASURED OBJECTIVE UP

Using the same technique as the Measured Objective Down except in reverse you take the measurement of A to B and add it on to C, it gives you D, the Measured Move Objective.

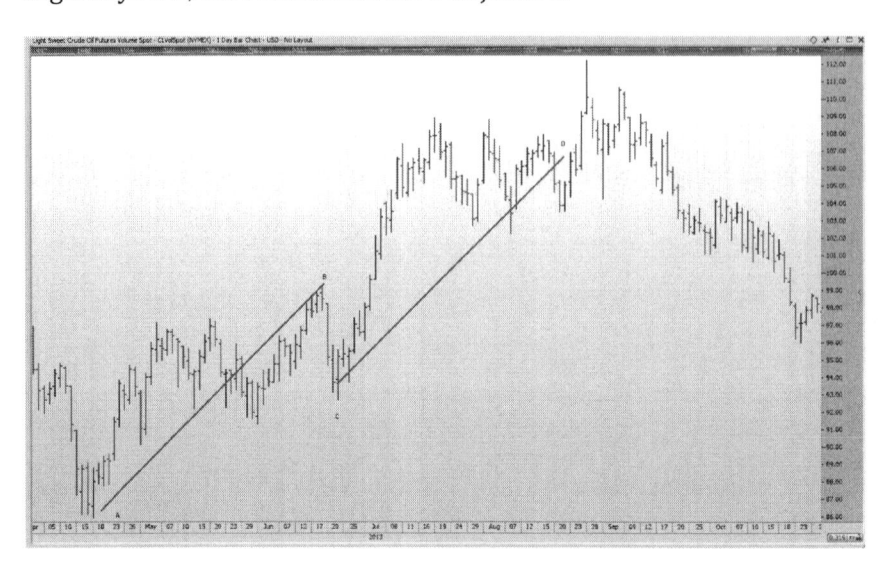

ONE-DAY REVERSAL

The one-day reversal is a signal that is usually good for a few days of a price move.

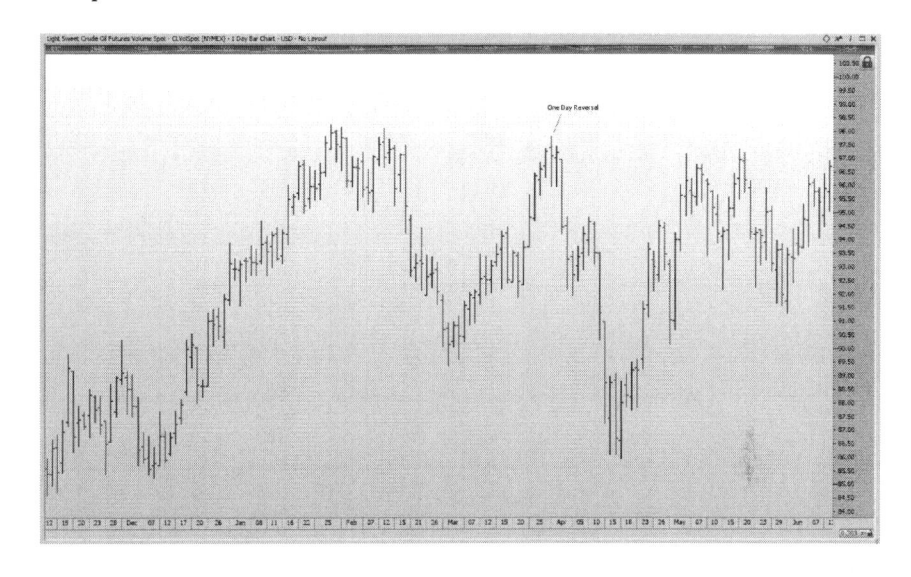

OUTSIDE BAR

The outside bar is a bar that has a higher high and lower low than the day before. Just like the inside, it will many times give a price reversal that lasts a few days. You should go with the breakout in the direction of the move. Other techniques should be used with it for price projections.

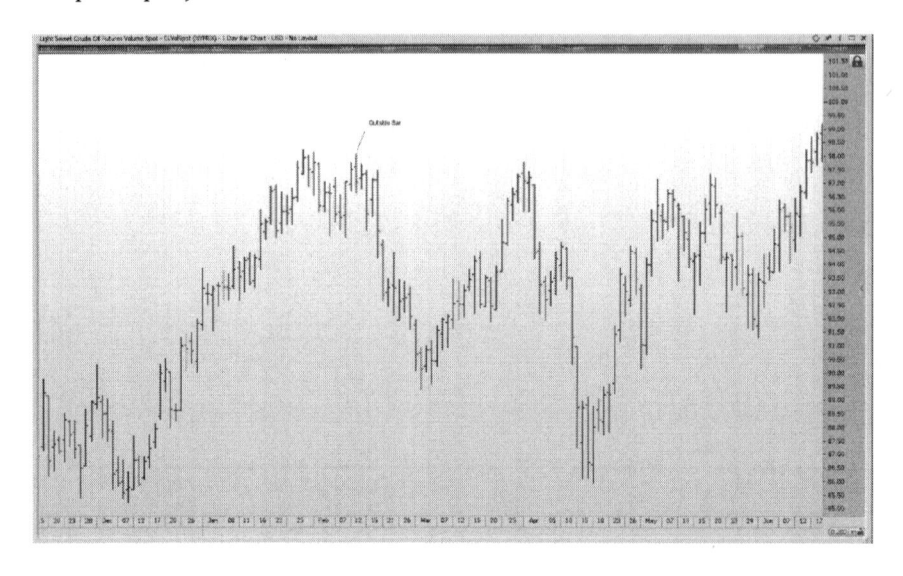

TWO REVERSE BARS

These are two adjacent bars stuck up or down out of the formation. They usually give a minor move in days.

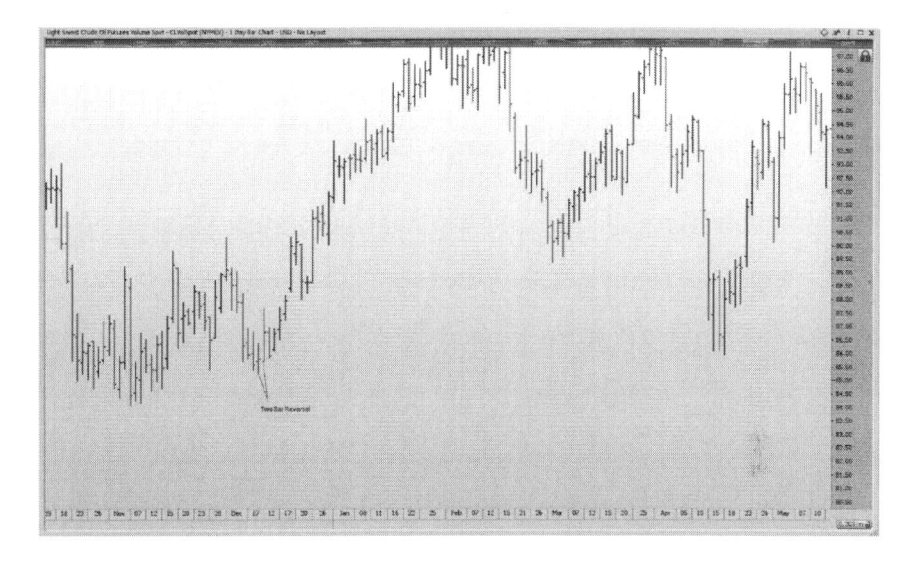

RECTANGLE BOTTOMS

Rectangle bottoms are very reliable. The longer the width the more reliable they are. It's best to have at least two touches on the top and bottom of the rectangle. In this case we had six touches. When the breakout first occurs, 90 percent of the time you will have a pullback to buy. The minimum objective is the height of the triangle. The maximum objective is the width of the rectangle. You can tie in other things like a near term pervious high and the objective of the ellipse.

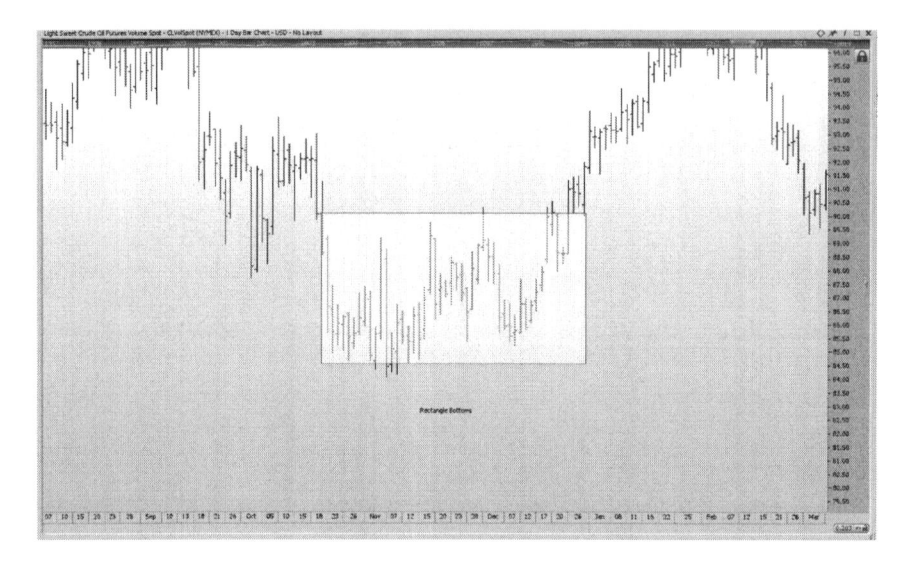

RECTANGLE TOPS

Here is an example of a rectangle top. It's just the reverse of the rectangle bottom. It needs at least 4 hits on the rectangle to make it valid. When the prices break down you then should short the first reaction. One objective is determined by the rectangle height, a second objective is determined by the triangle width. The previous low is another objective as well as the ellipse objective.

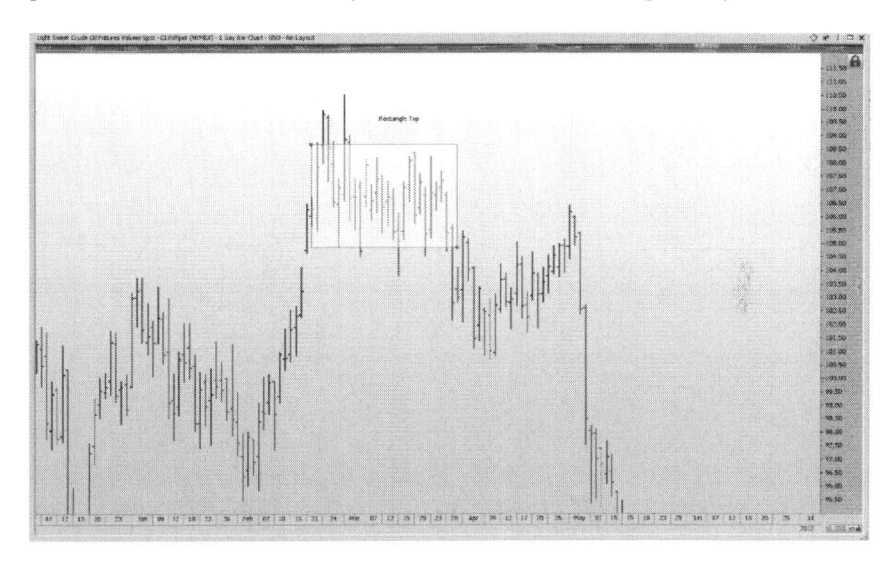

ROUNDED BOTTOM

The rounded bottom is a good signal. Normally you should wait for it to break out of the top of the rounded bottom. Buy the first reaction. The measured objective is the height of the rounded bottom added to its top.

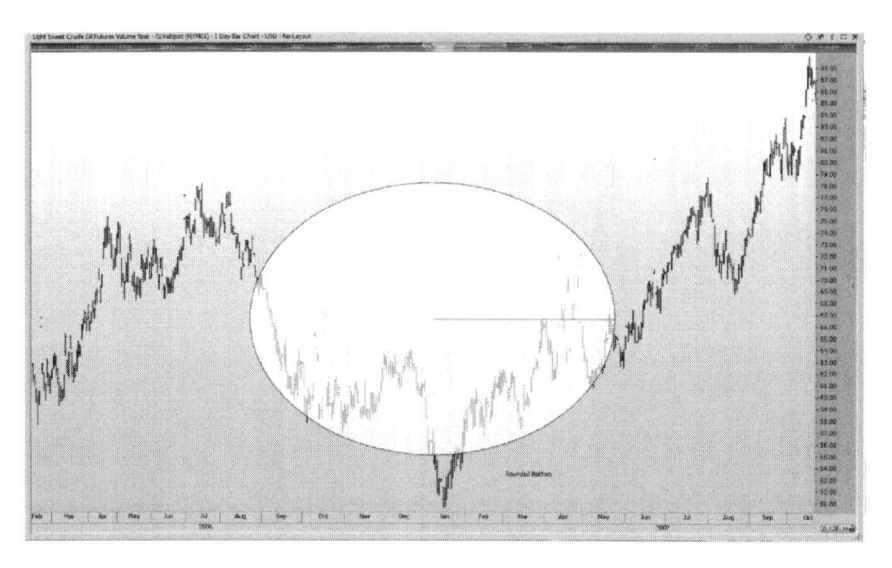

ROUNDED TOP

The rounded top is the opposite of the rounded bottom. Once the formation forms and breaks out under the bottom of the rounded top it can be shorted usually on a reaction. The measured objective is the distance from the top of the rounded top to the bottom added on to the bottom of the rounded top.

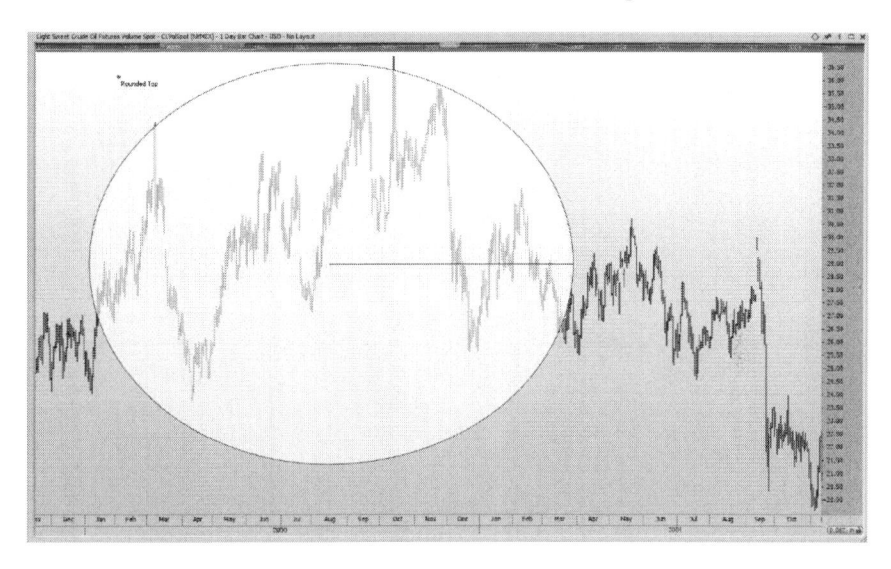

ELLIPSE UPTREND

This is a type upward move that fits into an ellipse. Try to buy at the first reaction of the ellipse and then exit at the break of the top of the ellipse.

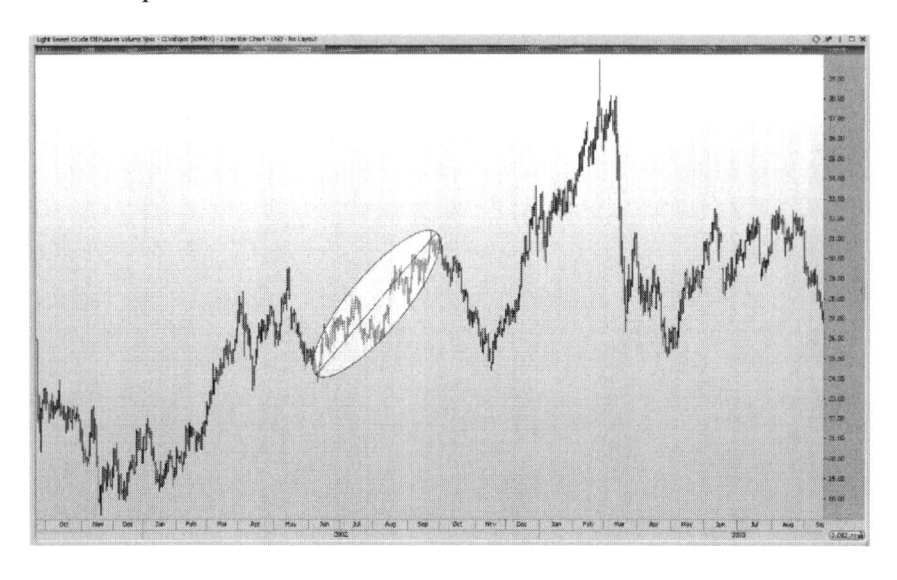

ELLIPSE DOWNTREND

You can also have an ellipse in a downtrend. Sell the first reaction in the ellipse and take profits at the bottom of the ellipse and prices breakout of it.

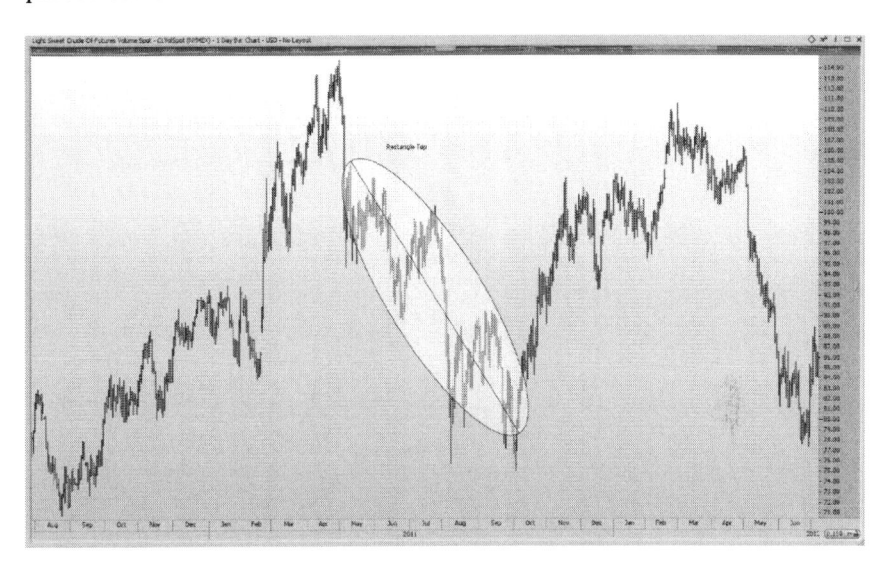

ASCENDING TRIANGLE

The ascending triangle is a very common formation in an uptrend. You need at least three points to hit in the formation. The next measured move is taken from the difference of the top of the triangle and the bottom of the triangle added to the breakout point of the triangle. It can also be bought when it breaks out of the triangle and has its first reaction.

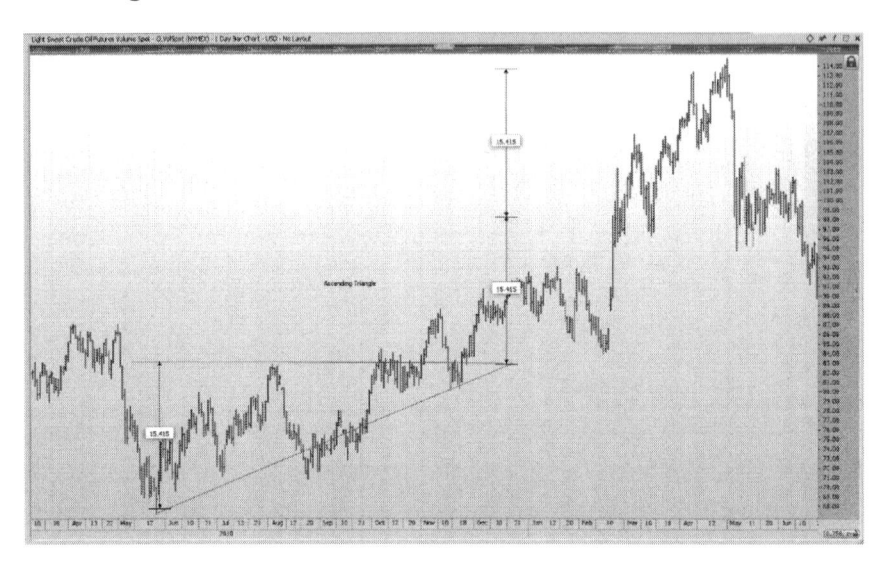

DESCENDING TRIANGLE

The descending triangle formation is the opposite of the ascending triangle formation with the same type of rules. In this case the market formed the descending triangle. It broke out on the downside. It could have been shorted on the break with the first reaction. It did not make its measured move initially, but it did make the ellipse projected move later on. Later on it also made it's descending triangle measured move.

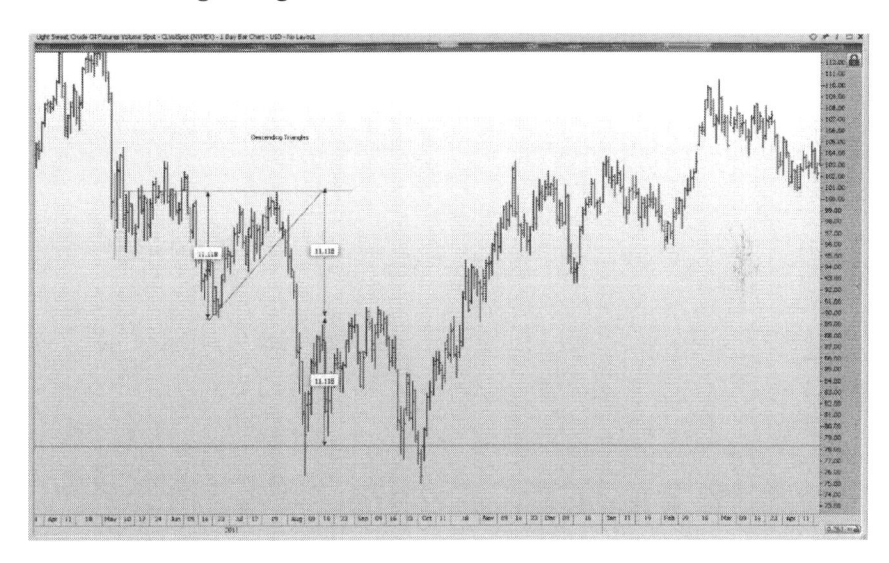

SYMMETRICAL TRIANGLES

The symmetrical bottom is a continuation triangle in the direction of the main trend. You can buy breakouts of the triangle in the direction of the trend. Buying the first reaction can also be done. Measured objectives can be taken from the breakout point using the high to low measurement of the triangle at point A.

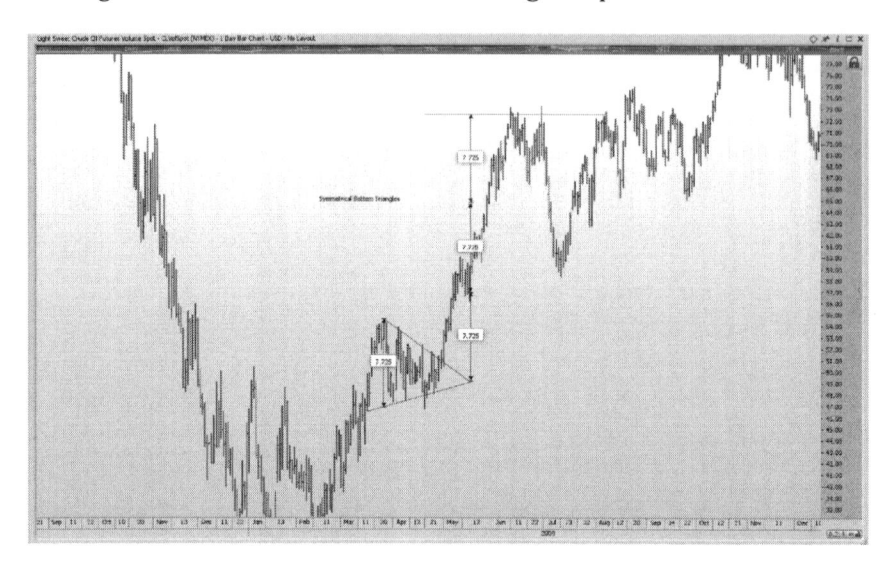

TRIPLE TOPS

Triple tops are excellent pattern formations. You can short the third high with a close stop. Follow the down move with a trailing stop.

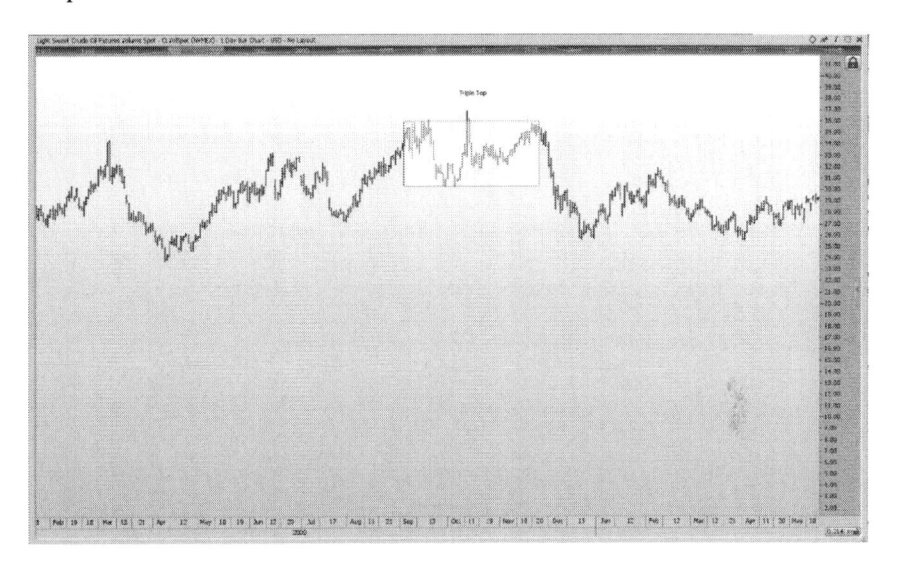

TRIPLE BOTTOMS

Triple bottoms are excellent pattern formations. The buy is a on the third bottom with a close stop. Follow the market up with a trialing stop.

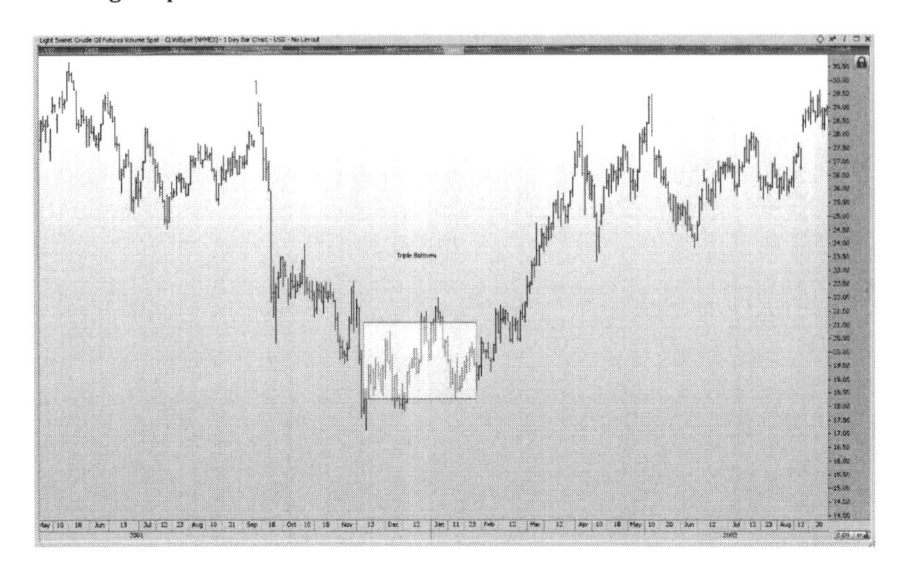

FALLING WEDGE

This is an excellent wedge formation, which has two downward slopping trend lines. It can be bought on a breakout of the downward slopping trend line after a slight reaction. Measured objective is taken from adding the widest part of the triangle added on to the breakout point. In this example the previous high was also an objective, which it did hit.

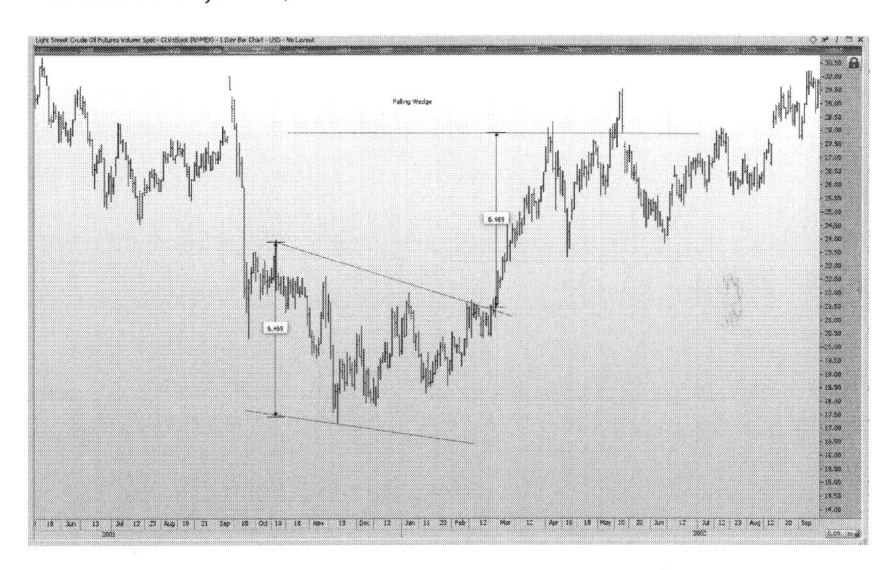

CHAPTER 10- WILLIAMS %R

How to use Williams %R a great momentum indicator! The formula for %R is:

{(highest high over? Periods – close)
/(highest high over? Periods -
lowest low over ? periods)} * - 100.

This is very complex. The good news is that it is available in most charting programs.

So what is Williams %R? It is a technical analysis oscillator that compares current price verses highs and lows. The oscillator is on a scale of 0 to100%.

The oscillator can be used in two different ways. Determine if a futures is overbought or oversold and it can be used as a momentum oscillator.

The person responsible for %R is Larry Williams. In 1987 he won the World Cup Championship of Futures Trading turning $10,000 into over $1.1 million dollars in 12 months using real money. Ten years later Michelle Williams won the same championship using Williams %R that her father won a decade earlier.

Generally a value of -80% or lower is oversold and a value of -20% or higher is overbought. These are general guidelines.

Larry Williams used a more sophisticated system. He would wait for the futures to reach negative 100% then have 5 trading days pass. If then %R reached above -95% or -85% he would buy. To go short the would wait for %R to reach 0% then wait 5 trading days to pass and have the %R to reach -5% or -15%.

The time periods used with this indicator is 10, 14 and 28.

The most consistent way to use the oscillator is if the indicator is overbought above -20 then falls back below -50 you can take this as a sign the market is moving lower. If the price was oversold below -80 and rallies above -50 take this as a sign the price will move higher.

Sometimes the indicator will give you false signals so hold all long positions as long the price is making higher swing lows. And remain short as long as the price is making lower swing highs.

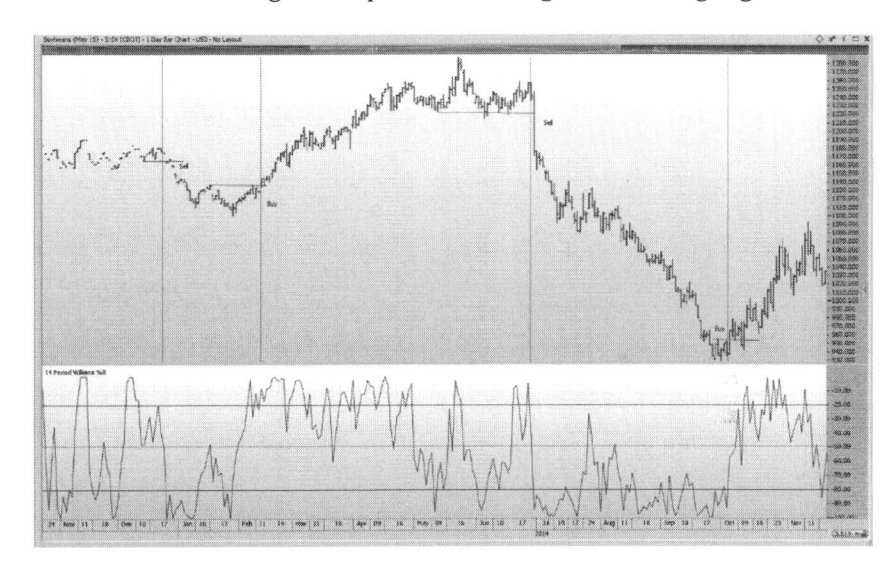

Chapter 11 - Long with Stops

The problem with indicators is they work sometimes but other times not. The reason is that the market is trending usually only 20% of the time and the rest of the time it is non-trending. Some indicators work in non-trending markets and other indicators work in trending markets. So there is no point in testing out indicators on long term historical markets say 5 years of data.

Perhaps the best way to enter a market is based on breakouts using the price patterns chapter in this book. Wait for a breakout then follow the market with a stop to protect gains. Using trailing stops many experts agree is a necessity. They limit losses and protect gains. But there are two problems using trailing stops.

1) One problem is that a sudden movement in a market due to a temporary market reaction to some possible news might just trigger an unwanted sell stop loss.

2) Another problem might be a big price gap down on the open between the close of the market of the prior day and the opening of the next day. This is usually due to some negative news. There is little that you can do about that.

Many traders use the simple moving average and apply that to a daily stop and they will put their stop a certain percentage below it from 1% up to 10%.

Another stop system many use is the Chandelier stop. It was introduced by Alexander Elder in his 2002 book Come into My Trading Room. It uses a multiple of the average true range from highs during an uptrend and then it adds them to lows during any down trend. See the following chart using the Chandelier stop on Soybeans. It is clear that Soybeans developed a head and shoulders top and broke the right neckline June 30th where it should have been shorted. Using the Chandelier stop it kept you short in the market till October 14th.

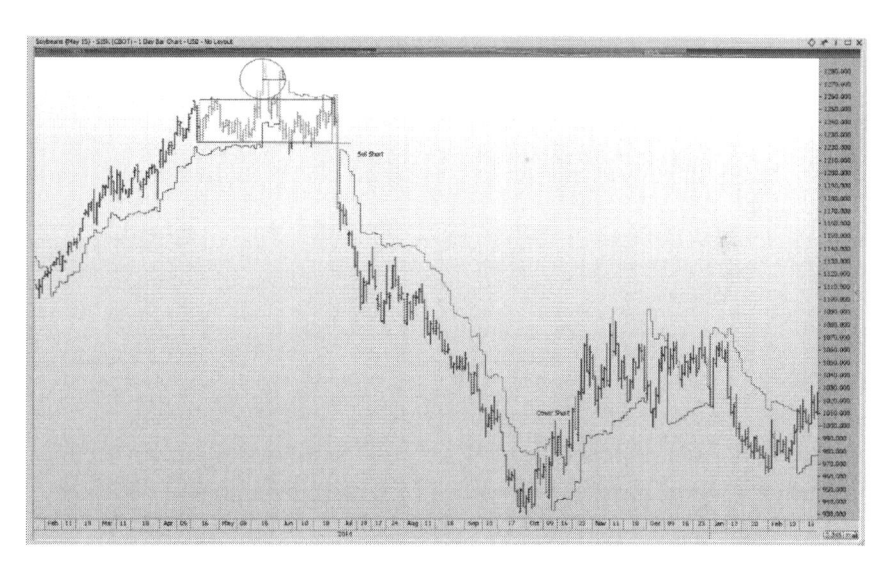

Chapter 12- KNOW YOURSELF

Is your negative life and potentially ruining your trading performance? You will never be happy with negative thoughts in your mind.

Here is an example:

Negative thought: I don't know how to handle what the market is doing right now?

Positive thought: This is my opportunity to learn how to trade this situation and learn something brand new.

When you are faced with conflicts you can come to terms with it and create a positive outcome.

You need to develop many switches to turn negatives into positives. This will empower yourself. Write down the switches and continue to repeat them daily. In your trading you will get many curve balls that will make things difficult and turning a negative into a positive may seems impossible, but you can do it. Have confidence in yourself. Eventually you will have a more positive attitude over time and will find much more satisfaction in your trading and in your life.

To stay motivated can be a daily concern but you need to think about the benefits you will reap by just incorporating this way of thinking. Positive will do this for you:

a) You will be a positive person

b) You will have more satisfaction in life

c) You will be pleasant to be around

d) You will be content

e) You will believe in successful trading

f) You will build successful trading skills

g) You will have ability to adapt to different trading situations

h) You will reduce your stress and that will help your long term health

i) Your positive behavior will be contagious to others around you and they will be positive to you.

You need to keep in mind that if you have been negative for a long time it won't be easy to turn this around. You may have many years of negative thoughts in your head. But you can program your brain to make it positive and successful in trading. To have positive thinking will take a lot of time and practice. You must change your thoughts if you want to be successful in trading.

You should get a journal and start recording your journey. Write down your positive thoughts and the barriers that you need to break through. You will find it is much easier each and every day to be positive over time. Then after a while all the negative thoughts will disappear leaving your mind with positive thoughts and your will be a more happy person, a successful person and enjoyable to be around.

Another thing that will help you is to surround yourself with positive and successful people. You are really the average of the people that you spend the most time with. So when you start this changing of your negative thoughts it is important that you have supportive and positive people around you.

Psychologists have written many articles on how important it is to surround you with positive people. People need to reinforce your positive attitude. The way to do this is to take stock of 20 people who know and then ask what was their disposition and how did they make you feel when you were around them. Was it supportive for you? Were they positive or negative?

Choose the people that were positive and try to spend more free time with them over the next 90 days. These people will be the key for you to change your negative thoughts. Only you can take the responsibility for changing your life. You need to think positively no matter what the situation is.

I have covered what I see for you to be a more positive and a successful trader. You can unleash the infinite power inside of yourself and be a successful trader by thinking positive. You should take at least 10 minutes every day to implement what you have learned in this chapter to be positive.

I trust that you will now take the action you need to change your attitude to being positive and leverage this into being a successful trader. You can achieve anything you want or desire. It is my hope that you will look inside of yourself and commit to being positive and get the freedom that you will gain by ending any habit of being a negative person.

Chapter 13 – Commitment of Traders Report

The Commitment of Traders Report is a report issued each Friday by the CFTC which shows the positions of commercial hedgers and large speculators in the different futures markets including the S&P and E-mini contracts. The report shows data with a 3-day lag. What is important is that it shows the positioning of the two largest participants in the market. This can provide you with some good insight for the direction of prices in the futures market. The participants are broken down into three categories. Number one is commercial hedgers, who are producers and users of commodities and they participate to lock in future prices or to protect against large moves in prices against them for the underlying commodity that they use. An example would be Nestles Chocolate who used futures price to hedge the price of Cocoa which they use to make their chocolate. Number two is large speculators who have futures positions above a certain size. They are required to report their holdings to the CFTC who then report that to the weekly Commitment of Traders Report. The position size level that requires reporting varies by market but to give you an idea; the reporting size for the S&P is 1,000 contracts. Number three is small speculators which is everyone not included in the above contracts. It is important to know that hedgers who don't meet the requirements above are also in this category.

So how can knowing these numbers give us an insight of how to trade the markets? Commercial hedgers often have a better insight of the direction of prices since they actually use the commodity. So one needs to look for movement out of the normal for this category as a tip where future prices might be headed. Normally commercial hedgers are the most bullish at market bottoms and the most bearish at market tops. So with this in mind looking at historical charts of the COT data at major tops and bottoms in historical price charts where it might be prudent to look for market reversals when looking at current market data.

Large speculators are normally trend followers and that means the more a commodity moves in one direction the more large speculators are going to be in that direction. When there are too many large speculators are in at an extreme either top or bottom that means the market may be nearing a reversal. If all of the large speculators are in the market there may not be any left to put on the trade in the direction of the trend. So if most large speculators are in one extreme position there may soon be a price reversal.

While the data for small speculators in not reported and because the data for the other two are it is easy to calculate the positions of the small speculators which are basically what is left over from the other two participants. Most do not look much at this third category because it includes both small speculators and small hedgers.

There is many different ways that this data can be used depending on your trading style. The above is meant as a general overview. To help you learn more about the Commitment of Traders Report follow the charts from the CME here.

http://www.cmegroup.com/tools-information/quikstrike/commitment-of-traders.html

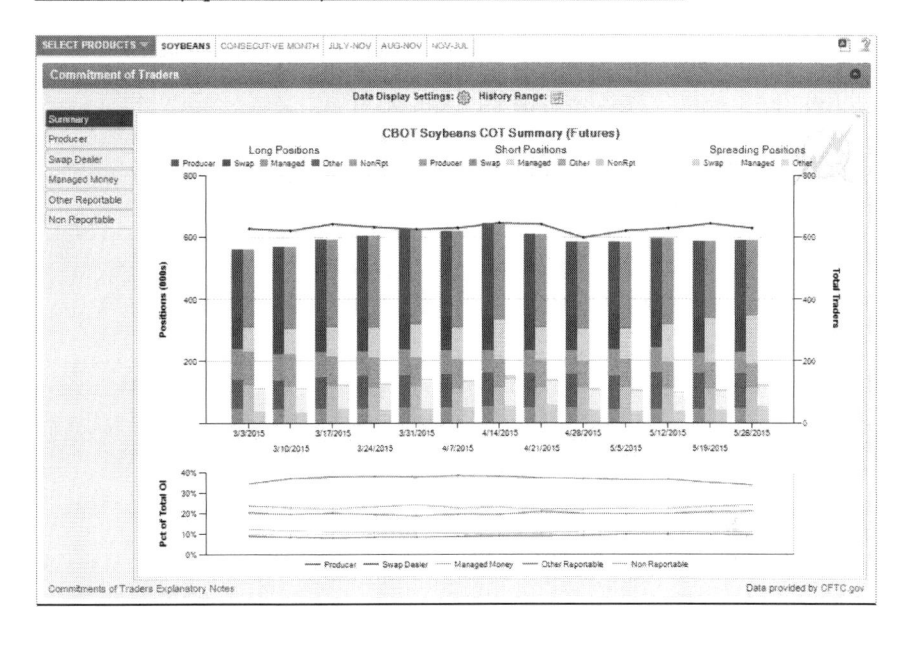

CHAPTER 14- MARKET-ANALYST

The Market-Analyst software is one of the finest technical analysis software packages in the world. It offers many technological innovations and technical indicators that most other charting software packages lack.

It is used by private traders, fund managers and professional analysts from across the globe. In most cases it is the technical analysis platform of their choice since it can do many things other packages simply can't do. It has many popular features and does include many proprietary models developed by many well-known market experts.

The Market-Analyst interface is built using very advanced graphics programing that gives you a fluid interface with powerful alluring data visualization techniques.

It uses both end of the day and real time data. The charts and the analysis all do updates and recalculations with every tick that comes in.

To arrange a FREE trial of Market Analyst 7 please go to:

http://www.mav7.com/lp/tradersworld/?cname=TRADERSWOR

or go here:

http://www.worldcupadvisor.com/MichaelTrading.html

Chapter 15- WORLD CUP ADVISOR

About http://www.worldcupadvisor.com/

Talented professionals from around the world display their live futures and forex trading accounts in real time on WCA and allow subscribers to follow their activity. You can follow the trading of any WCA lead account automatically in your own account with World Cup AutoTrade service. Program features include:

Transparency:

All trades displayed on WorldCupAdvisor.com are actual trades in funded accounts unless otherwise noted. Details of every round-turn trade made in every available account are shown in the Advisor Performance section; for a free login, complete the "Create Your FREE Guest Login" form on the home page. Profit/loss in the Advisor Performance section is shown exclusive of commissions, fees, transaction and subscription costs; to evaluate the impact of these trading overhead costs, click the Net-Profit Calculator link. Detailed Performance Reports are also available within the Advisor Performance section. Read about each advisor and the specifications of his lead ("Live Update") accounts in the Advisors section. Our lead traders compete with each other to earn customer trust and subscription business.

Clarity:

Subscribers have access to a real-time display of activity in the lead account(s) to which they are subscribed. Displays feature separate screens for orders entered, open positions, closed positions and advisor commentary (please note that some order screens are disabled upon request of the advisor). When you're logged into a Live Update program, an instant message will appear on your screen and a bell will ring any time there is new activity. An email notification also accompanies each new activity, and subscribers can also receive text message notifications if desired at no additional charge.

Flexibility:

Subscriptions are sold on a month-to-month basis, eliminating long-term commitments. With AutoTrade service, subscribers can start a new program or stop an existing one with a single phone call. Subscribers can control their own leverage by adjusting funding levels and adding or reducing exposure to a variety of programs.

Diversification:

The wide variety of WCA accounts gives investors the opportunity to diversify across asset classes, trading products and strategies. Please note, however, that diversification in not necessarily available when trading a single program. Click here to learn more about ways you can diversify your WCA investments. A prospect should evaluate each specific program's specifications to determine whether or not that program is suitable to the individual based on that person's diversification requirements. Monthly subscriptions are sold separately for each program.

Confidence:

We try hard to identify traders we believe are capable of sustaining profitable performance on a net basis over time. Many of our advisors have posted top finishes in the prestigious World Cup Trading Championships®. We also feature accounts traded by noted system developers, authors, commentators and educators. The WCA live trading "incubator" is an active testing ground for new programs. WCA AutoTrade service is designed to deliver same-price fills for leader and followers alike on futures trades; authorized brokers will waive commissions on any WCA leader-follower trade in which a follower's fill price is not equal to or better than the lead trader's fill price (with the exception of trades placed outside a program's AutoTrade block when synchronizing positions for a follower entering a program or liquidating positions for a follower exiting a program).

Risk and suitability:

It is important to remind you that trading futures and forex involves significant risk of loss and is not suitable for everyone. Following any of our lead accounts should be undertaken with risk capital only. Before investing, you should carefully consider your risk tolerance and suitability for this type of investment.

Support:

We're here to answer your questions and provide a personal tour of the site if desired. Contact us by email at info@worldcupadvisor.com or by phone at 1-312-454-5000 or 1-877-456-7111.

CHAPTER 16- OTHER TRADERS WORLD BOOKS

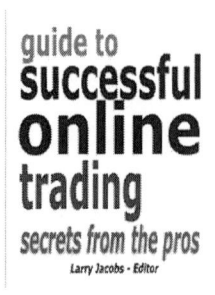

Guide to Successful Online Trading: Secrets from the Pros

http://www.amazon.com/Guide-Successful-Online-Trading-Secrets-ebook/dp/B00QOBED34

This is one of the finest trading books you'll ever see about trading. The reason is that it comes from a group of expert pro traders with multiple years of experience.

Trading as you know is extremely difficult. It is estimated that 90% of traders lose money in the markets. To help you overcome this statistic, the pro traders in this book give you their ideas on trading with some of the best trading methods ever developed through their long time experience. By reading about these trading methods and implementing them in the markets you will then have a chance to then join the ranks of the 10% of the successful traders.

The traders in this book have through experience the right attitude and employ a combination of technical analysis principles and strategies to be successful. You can develop these also.

Trading is one of the best ways to make money. Apply the trading methods in this book and treat it as a business. The purpose of this book is to help you be successful in trading.

From this book you will get all the strategies, Indicators and trading methods that you need to make big profits in the markets.

This book gives you:

1) Audio/Visual Links to presentations from pro traders

2) The best strategies that the professional traders are using now

3) The broad perspective you need in today's difficult markets

4) The Exact tools that you need to make profitable trading decisions

5) The finest trading education

I wish to express my appreciation to all the writers in this book who made the book possible. They have spent many hours of their time and hard work in writing their section of the book and the putting together their video presentation for the online expo.

Trade the Markets with an Edge: Use Your Mind

http://www.amazon.com/Trade-Markets-Traders-World-Online-ebook/dp/B00KTQJV50

If you don't have the mind of a top trader, this book might be able to help you develop one. The writers in this book are very experienced and they are here to help you to be successful. Each of them has their own expertise in trading. What you need to do is to read the entire book and find the trader that fits your own trading style and grab it and make it your own. It is just that simple.

Find Success

This book presents to you the best trading strategies of these traders so that you might be able to select those that fit you best and then implement them into your own trading style.

In this book you'll learn:

1) How these expert traders make money and why

2) How to develop your own trading strategy

3) How to improve your trading psychology

4) How to be the trader you always wanted to be. You'll also learn how to avoid the losers and get rid of emotional attachment to trades. To be successful you need to learn to dump the losers quickly and keep the winners for big moves. Another thing this book does it that it gives you the desire to make continuous profits just like the master traders do.

Making profits one after another gives you a fantastic feeling which is tremendous!

Tips for Success

Also in this book you will know who to listen to for ideas from people who have many years of experience and who are seasoned traders.

Crucial Factors

In this book learn about crucial factors in the markets that many experts won't tell you about regarding time, volume and little known indicators. You'll know the right factors that can make you a profitable trader. The unique viewpoints from these many traders can explain why many traders lose and that can help you. The book was designed to help you develop your own trading edge in the markets to put you above others who don't have an edge and just trade by the seat of their pants.

Best Trading Strategies

http://www.amazon.com/Best-Trading-Strategies-Futures-Markets-ebook/dp/B00GG94F78

This is one of the most fascinating books that was ever written about trading because it is written by over thirty expert traders. These traders have many years of experience and they have learned how to turn technical analysis into profits in the markets. This is extremely difficult to do and if you have ever tried to trade the markets with technical analysis you would know what I mean. These writers have some of the best trading strategies they use and have the conviction and the discipline to act assertively and pull the buy or sell trigger regardless of pressures they have against them. They have presented these strategies at the Traders World Online Expo #14 in video presentations and in this book.

What sets these traders apart from other traders? Many think that beating the markets has something to do with discovering and using some secret formula. The traders in this book have the right attitude and many employ a combination of fundamental analysis, technical analysis principles and formulas in their best trading strategies.

Trading is one of the best ways to make a lot of money in the world if one does it right. One needs to find successful trading strategies and implement them in their own trading method. The purpose of this book is to present to you the best trading strategies of these traders so that you might be able to select those that fit you best and then implement them into your own trading.

I wish to express my appreciation to all the writers in this book who made the book possible. They have spent many hours of their time and hard work in writing their section of the book and the putting together their video presentation for the online expo.

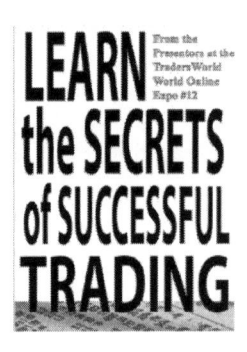

Learn the Secrets of Successful Trading

http://www.amazon.com/Secrets-Successful-Trading-Traders-Online-ebook/dp/B00A2ZIJQ0

Learn specific trading strategies to improve your trading, learn trading ideas and tactics to be more profitable, better optimize your trading system, find the fatal flaws in your trading, understand and use Elliott Wave to strengthen your trading, position using correct sizing to trade more profitable, understand Mercury cycles in trading the S&P, get consistently profitable trade setups, reduce risk and increase profits using volume, detect and trade the hidden market cycles, short term trading by taking the money and running, develop your mind for trading, overcoming Fear in Trading, trade with the smart money following volume, understand and use the Ultimate Oscillator, use high power trading with geometry, get better entries, understand the three legs to trading, use technical analysis with NinjaTrader 7, use a breakout system with cycles for greater returns with less risk, use Turn Signal for better entries and exits, trade with an edge, use options profitably, learn to trade online, map supply and demand on charts, quantify and execute portfolio rotation for auto trading.

Written by Many Expert Traders

The book was written by a large group of 35 expert traders, with high qualifications, most of who trade professionally and/or offer trading services and expensive courses to their clients. Some of them charge thousands of dollars per day for personal trading! These expert traders give generally 45-minute presentations covering the same topics given in this book at the Traders World Online Expo #12. By combining their talents in this book, they introduce a new dimension to finding a profitable trading edge in the market. You can use ideas and techniques of this group of experts to leverage your ability to find an edge to successfully trade. Using a group of experts in this manner to insure your trading success is unprecedented.

You'll never find a book like this anywhere! This unique trading book will help you uncover the underlying reasons for your lack of consistency in trading and will help you overcome poor habits that cost you money in trading. It will help you to expose the myths of the market one by one teaching you the right way to trade and to understand the realities of risk and to be comfortable with trading with market. The book is priceless!

Parallels to the Traders World Online Expo 12

The articles in this book exactly parallel the video presentations given at the Traders World Online Expo #12. This expo joins these top trading experts together with active traders looking for trading strategies & specific recommendations to help them profit in the markets and is held online at TradersWorldOnlineExpo.com.

From the DVD you'll learn: Time and Price Points; Consistently Profitable Trade Setups; How to Control Fear of Trading; Detecting and Trading Hidden Market Cycles; Position Sizing; Detailed Analysis of the S&P Market, 3 Keys to be a System Trader, Trading with an Edge, Lift off Trading Systems, Monetizing your Trading Expertise; Tracking Smart Money; Trading Price Cycles, Using Options, Mastering Trading with NinjaTrader; Learning Andrews Trading and much more.

Finding Your Trading Method

http://www.amazon.com/Finding-Trading-Method-Traders-Online-ebook/dp/B00DAIOL0E

Finding your trading method is the main problem you need to solve if you want to become a successful trader. You may be asking yourself, can I find my own trading method that will reflect my own personality toward trading? For example, do you have the patience to sit in front of a computer and trade all day? Do you prefer to swing trade from 3-5 days or do you like to hold positions for weeks and even months? Every trader is different. You need to find your own trading method.

Finding out your trading method is extremely important to produce a profitable benchmark that can be replicated in your live account. Perhaps the best way to find a successful trading method is to listen to many expert traders to understand what they have done to be successful. The best way to do that is to listen to the Traders World Online Expos presentations. This book duplicates what these experts have said in their presentations, which explains what they have done to find their own trading method.

If you have a trading method that gives you a predictable profit, then that type of objectivity contributes to your trading edge. The problem with most traders is that being inconsistent will never allow them to have an edge. After you find your trading method that you feel comfortable with, you must have the following:

An overall plan to:

1) Set your rule set and plan and then stick with it in all of your trading.

2) To give you a trading plan for every day.

The trade plan then should:

1) Have an exact entry price

2) Have a stop price

3) Have a way to add positions

4) Tell you where to take profits

5) Have a way to protect your profits

By reviewing all the methods given in this book by the expert traders, it will give, you the preliminary steps that you need to find your footing in finding your own trading method.

Reading this book and by seeing the actual recorded presentations on the Traders World Online Expo site can act as a reference tool for selecting your method of trading, investment strategies and tactics.

It took many of these expert traders in this book 15 – 30 years to finally come up and find the answers to find their trading method to make consistent profit. Finding your trading method could be then much easier when you read this book and incorporate the techniques that best fit your personality and style from these traders. This book will enable you to that fastest way to do that.

So if you want help to find your own trading method to be successful in the markets then buy and read this book.

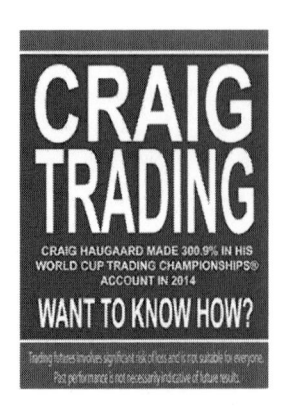

CRAIG TRADING: Craig Haugaard made 300.9% in his World Cup Trading Championships® Account in 2014 - Want to Know How?

http://www.amazon.com/CRAIG-TRADING-Haugaard-Trading-Championships%C2%AE-ebook/dp/B00WT2CO7Y

This book contains an interview that I made with Craig Haugaard, third-place finisher in the 2014 World Cup Championship of Futures Trading® with a 300.9% net profit. I asked him many questions on exactly how he did it.

In the rest of the book I explain to you how to use the indicators that Craig used to make his 300.9% return.

Here are the indicators that he used:

• Seasonality

• MACD

• Stochastics

- Moving Averages

- Trailing Stops

- Fibonacci Retracements & Extensions

All of the charts in this book are produced using my favorite charting software Market-Analyst®. I have also arranged for you to get a FREE trial so that you might have the chance to actually work with these indicators with a real charting platform.

You will also be able to view the video presentations that I personally created so you can see how these indicators can be setup and followed with clear and concise step-by-step instructions.

> Market-Analyst
> Moving Averages
> Cycles
> Seasonality
> Volume
> Patterns
> Williams %R
> Chandelier Stops

After you understand how these indicators work, I would then recommend that you go to WorldCupAdvisor.com and consider following Michael Cook's real-time trades.

This one-of-a-kind book teaches you how to identify the direction of the markets and trade the markets by using popular trading indicators. This is done by concise instructions backed by learning videos, hands on practice with real trading software and by following real-time trades of a master trader.

CHAPTER 17 - 2015 WORLD CUP TRADING CHAMPIONSHIPS® SPONSORS:

ONLINE TRADING ACADEMY

http://www.tradingacademy.com

OTA is the world's most trusted name in financial education for stocks, forex, futures and options.

APEX INVESTING INSTITUTE

http://apexinvesting.com

THE source for how to trade Futures, Forex, CFD's and NADEX Binaries and Spreads

TRADE NAVIGATOR

http://www.tradenavigator.com

The Trade Navigator Trading Platform takes immense quantities of complex data and distills it down to what really matters.

THE BUBBA SHOW

http://thebubbashow.org

Learn the intricacies of options trading from Todd "Bubba" Horwitz, educator, trading coach and author OF "AVERAGE JOE OPTIONS."

WORLDCUPADVISOR.COM

http://www.worldcupadvisor.com

Automatically mirror the trading of futures and forex professionals with World Cup Leader-Follower AutoTrade™ service.

NINJATRADER

http://www.ninjatrader.com

Award-winning software that benefits all levels of traders with trade management advanced charting, market analytics, customizable features and more.

ABOUT THE AUTHOR

Larry Jacobs has a B.S. and Master's Degree in Business and has been editor of Traders World Magazine since 1988. It's a leading financial magazine which has both classical and modern technical analysis articles as well as reviews of the latest trading books, trading computer hardware and software.

He also has written dozens of articles on how to setup your home trading office and how to get the right trading computer.

He is author of several trading books including Gann Masters, Gann Masters II, Gann Master Charts Unveiled, Patterns and Ellipses and W. D. Gann in Real Time Trading. Gann Masters was so popular it was recently translated in to Italian.

He has reviewed almost every trading software program available and has interviewed and talked to the many of leading traders of the world.

He won the World Cup Championship of Stock Trading® in 2001.

DISCLAIMER

This publication is intended to provide helpful and informative material. It is not intended to give trading recommendations nor is it to replace the advice of a financial advisor. No action should be taken solely on the contents of this book. Always consult your financial advisor on any matters regarding your investing or trading before adopting any suggestions in this book or drawing inferences from it.

The author and publisher specifically disclaim all responsibility for any liability, loss or risk, personal or otherwise, which is incurred as a consequence, directly or indirectly, from the use or application of any contents of this book.

Any and all product names referenced within this book are the trademarks of their respective owners. None of these owners have sponsored, authorized, endorsed, or approved this book.

Always read all information provided by the manufacturers' product labels before using their products. The author and publisher are not responsible for claims made by manufacturers.

Trading futures and forex involves significant risk of loss and is not suitable for everyone. Past performance is not necessarily indicative of future results. There is unlimited risk of loss in selling options. An investor must read, understand and sign a Letter of Direction for WCA programs before investing. There are no guarantees of profit no matter who is managing your money. Net-profit data under "Leaders to Follow" and "Top Net

Performers" includes open trade equity if any as of market close on the date listed, and is calculated using current WCA subscription rates, standardized commission rates (including Exchange fees but not NFA fees) and funding requirements available through any authorized AutoTrade broker. For detail on commission calculations, open the Net-Profit Calculator. Trades displayed on WorldCupAdvisor.com are from proprietary accounts that are either owned by the advisor or are entities of which the advisor is a beneficial owner. Performance data shown for lead accounts is not necessarily indicative of subscriber rate of return and drawdown due to execution, slippage, subscriber funding level and other factors. While great care is taken in the preparation of information presented on WCA, subscribers must rely on their account statements for subscriber-specific performance of any WCA program. WCA accounts do not necessarily represent all the accounts controlled by the advisor. The advisor may have other accounts that may be subject to commission rates different than rates required to follow his or her WCA account with AutoTrade service and may produce results different than his or her WCA account(s). The advisor may have previously displayed other accounts on WCA. Accounts trading in the World Cup Trading Championships (WCC) do not necessarily represent all the WCC accounts controlled by the competitor, may be subject to commission rates different than rates required to follow a WCC account with AutoTrade service, and may produce results different than the results achieved in other WCC accounts of the competitor. To view the trade-by-trade history of all WCA programs in our "Performance" section, fill out the "Performance Reports" form on the WorldCupAdvisor.com home page.

Also please note: That Halliker's, Inc. the publisher of this book is an affiliate of both World Cup Advisor and Market-Analyst.

COPYRIGHT

Copyright© 2015 by Halliker's, Inc.

All rights reserved, including the right to reproduce the book or portions thereof in any form whatsoever. For information address:

Halliker's, Inc.
2508 W. Grayrock St.
Springfield, MO 65810

Manufactured in the United States of America

Printed in Great Britain
by Amazon.co.uk, Ltd.,
Marston Gate.